Oriental Libraries
of India and their Collections

Oriental Libraries
of India and their Collections

By

Dr. Amjad Ali
Deputy Librarian
Aligarh Muslim University, Aligarh
&
Chairman
Central Sectional Committee for Oriental Libraries
Indian Library Association, New Delhi

Ess Ess Publications

4837/24, Ansari Road, Darya Ganj,
New Delhi-110002
✆ : 23260807
Fax : 23274173
E-mail: info@essessreference.com
url:http://www.essessreference.com

First Published 2004

ISBN : 81-7000-416-0

Price : Rs. 450/-

Published by :

Ess Ess Publications

4837/24, Ansari Road, Darya Ganj,
New Delhi - 110 002
Phone : 23260807
Fax : 23274173
E-mail: info@essessreference.com
url:http://www.essessreference.com

Printed at :

Mehra Offset Press, New Delhi.

Dedicated to my Wife

Zohra

for the inspiration to write

Contents

PREFACE

Through out the ages, India remained a rich country both culturally and economically. Its contribution to knowledge is next to none. Learning was an established tradition here for quite a large number of people for a long time. The records of knowledge were created and preserved for the posterity in scientific ways. The vast amount of information resources available through out the country in varied forms tell the fascinating stories of its glorious past.

The richness of the country invited invasions by Indo-Aryans, Greeks, Arabs, Persians, Englishmen etc. which left a great impression on its social, economic and cultural life affecting the languages of masses. The Indo-Aryan vernaculars were influenced by languages altogether strange to India and contact with the tongues of aliens affected their vocabularies to a great extent and also created new languages.

The foreign rulers in India took special interest in collecting the records of knowledge, especially manuscripts available on palm leaves and paper. They took great care of this cultural treasure. As a tradition they established private libraries in their palaces. It was because of their efforts that most of the records have been saved and known to the entire World. It is also ture that a large number of valuable books and manuscripts have been taken out of the country during the political upheavals, still the resources collected and saved by some enthusiastic persons of the country form a treasure trove. As the time goes by, newer resources come into light and are introduced to the people.

My intension in writing this book was to collect information about the holdings of Oriental libraries irrespective of their locations or languages of availability and to bring together their details. Many sources including books available in English, Urdu

and Hindi languages as well as the relevant Internet websites have been consulted for this work. It was found that the information in books was outdated in most of the cases whereas the same available on Internet was too short to present a comprehensive picture. Therefore, the approach adopted for this book was to collect relevant materials from all the available sources and to present it in a way that the gap between the old and the new is bridged and a comprehensive picture of Oriental libraries is formed.

It was not possible to cover all the oriental libraries of the country in a single volume in view of their large number. Therefore, only a few major libraries have been taken up and studied in detail. Utmost care has been taken to present facts in order to maintain accuracy and reliability of data presented in the book but it cannot be said to be perfact in all respect. The author will be highly thankful for suggestions to improve and update the work and the suggestion in this regard will be duly acknowledged and incorporated in the next edition.

I am highly indebted to a number of persons who have helped me in writing this book and also the authors of books and managers of websites whose materials I have consulted in this connection. My thanks are also due to M/s Ess Ess Publications, New Delhi who brought out the book in a very short time.

Dr. Amjad Ali

amjad_alig@yahoo.co.in

1

THE ASIATIC SOCIETY LIBRARY, KOLKATTA

The Asiatic Society is a premier oriental institution of the country. It was founded in 1784 by Sir William Jones (1746-1794) who dreamt of a centre for Asian studies including almost everything concerning man and nature within the geographical limits of the continent - the history, civil and natural, the antiquities, arts, sciences and literature of Asia. In the dim hours of the genesis of the Asiatic Society, William Jones for all his efforts could not procure even a slice of land wherein to house his Asian dream. The Society which in no time was to be regarded as the first and best of its kind in the whole world had no permanent address, no fixed place for holding its meetings and, which was most disconcerting, no funds.

Sir William Jones arrived in Calcutta on 25 September 1783 as a Puisne Judge of the Old Supreme Court.While still on board of the frigate Crococlile carrying him from England to India, he prepared a memorandum detailing his plan of study. This included 'the laws of the Hindus and Mahomedans; the history of the ancient world; proofs and illustrations of scripture; traditions concerning the deluge; modern politics and geography of Hindusthan; Arithmatic and Geometry and mixed sciences of Asiaticks; Medicine, Chemistry, Surgery and Anatomy of the Indians; natural products of India; poetry, rhetoric and morality of Asia; music of the Eastern nations; the best accounts of Tibet and Kashmir; trade, manufactures, agriculture and commerce of India: Mughal constitution, Marhatta constitution etc. This memorandum could easily be regarded as an early draft of the memorandum of the Asiatic Society itself. The Society which

was still in the embryo of a dream was actually born within four months of Jones's arrival in India.

William Jones was, however, not the earliest among the Orientalists of the East India Company to arrive in India. About a decade earlier came Charles Wilkins (1770), Nathaniel Brassey Halhed (1772) and Jonathan Duncan (1772):Warren Hastings's "bright young men",who had paved the way for the two future institutions- The Asiatic Society and the College at Fort William. All the Orientalists who became famous in history clustered around either the Society or the College or both. The Society, of course, was the pioneer and first in the field.

While others were thinking in terms of individual study and research, Sir William Jones was the first man to think in terms of a permanent organisation for Oriental studies and researches on a grand scale in this country. He took the initiative and in January 1784 sent out a circular letter to selected persons of the elite with a view to establishing a Society for this purpose. In response to his letter, thirty European gentlemen of Calcutta including Mr. Justice Hyde, John Carnac, Henry Vansittart, John Shore, Charles Wilkins, Francis Gladwin, Jonathan Duncan and others gathered on 15 January 1784 in the Grand Jury Room of the old Supreme Court of Calcutta. The Chief Justice Sir Robert Chambers presided at the first meeting and Jones delivered his first discourse in which he put forward his plans for the Society.

Asia, he said, was the "nurse of sciences" and the "inventress of delightful and useful arts." He proposed to found a Society under the name of The Asiatick Society. The name went through a number of changes like The Asiatick Society (1784-1825), The Asiatic Society (1825-1832), The Asiatic Society of Bengal (1832-1935), The Royal Asiatic Society of Bengal (1936-1951) and The Asiatic Society again since July 1951.

In the first meeting, the Governor-General, Warren Hastings was elected Patron and Sir William Jones the President. The Memorandum of Articles of Society read as follows: "The

bounds of its investigations will be the geographical limits of Asia, and within these limits its enquiries will be extended to whatever is performed by MAN or produced by NATURE." Later, in his famous Third Annual Discourse, Jones emphasised the superiority of Sanskrit as a language: "The Sanskrit language, whatever be its antiquity, is of a wonderful structure, more perfect than the Greek, more copious than the Latin and more exquisitely refined than either."

The pioneering activity of the Society was praised abroad and even compared with that of the Italian Humanists of the quattrocento. But the first two decades of the Society's existence remained precarious. The original plan of holding meetings every week had to be discarded, and even monthly meetings were not possible. When William Jones died in 1794, the Society was just an orphan of ten, having no roof overhead and no assured funds to defray normal running expenses, not to speak of having in its proud possession, as it has today, an invaluable Asokan rock edict or precious old coins. There was hardly any hint at that time that Jones's dream of a world centre of Oriental studies in Calcutta was going to survive.

In 1805 the Government gifted to the Society a plot of land at the corner of Park Street and Chowringhee, the present site of the Asiatic Society, to which was added later, in 1849, a small portion on the western side. The construction of the Society's own building on the plot was completed in 1808, and the books, papers and records that had accumulated over the years could get a permanent shelter. Years rolled on, and with the expansion of the activities of the Society the problem of accommodation was acutely felt. But no solution was forthcoming till after India's Independence. As late as 1961, thanks to the generous helps of the Government of India and the Government of West Bengal, the construction of a new building was started in the premises of the Society to solve the problem of space, and the new four-storeyed building was formally opened by Dr. S. Radhakrishnan, the then President of India, on 22 February 1965.

Membership of the Society for many years remained exclusively European, and only in January 1829, on the suggestion of Dr. Horace Hayman Wilson, Indian members were for the first time admitted to the Society. The earliest Indian members of the Society were Prasanna Kumar Tagore, Dwarkanath Tagore, Russamay Dutt and Ram Camul Sen. It was not until December 1832 that Radhakanta Deb was invited to become a member.

In the beginning, the Society was very loosely organised and had no real Executive Body. It had only two important functionaries: a President who conducted meetings, and a Secretary who kept the minutes. After Jones's death the interest of the members declined considerably and in 1800 a resolution had to be passed urging members to attend meetings more regularly. Financial conditions were so bad, and there were so many defaulters among the members, that the first Treasurer of the Society, Henry Trail resigned in desperation in 1799. After the turn of the century things began to look up.

The vacuum created by the death of Jones led to the institutionalisation of the Society more rapidly. Regular admission and membership fees, and annual election of a Treasurer and two Vice-Presidents were introduced, and a proposal for the construction of Society's own building was made on 29 September1796 to Sir John Shore, President of the Society, who was also the Governor-General. The next Governor-General, Lord Wellesley took steps to coordinate between the works of the Society and those of the College at Fort William, and on 2 April 1800 John Gilchrist, Professor at the College of Fort William, was made Secretary of the Society. As the Society began to function more institutionally, the post of Secretary assumed new importance, second to that of the President. After Gilchrist, the two illustrious Secretaries were H. H. Wilson and James Prinsep. Gilchrist movd energetically in the matter of the construction of building for the Society and in 1808 when at last the Society had its own building, the Asiatic Society became the

first fully equipped, established institution in the world for Asian studies.

Asiatic Society and Fort William College

The collaboration between the Society and the Fort William College increased, and this collaboration was symbolised in 1807 when Henry Colebrooke became the President of the College Council as well as the President of the Asiatic Society. Already in 1805 the Secretary of the Society, William Hunter had been made the Secretary of the College. In 1808 Colebrooke as President of the College transferred a section of the Fort William College Library to the Society.

The publication of the Asiatick Researches became assured when Hunter's Hindoostan Press took up its printing responsibility. Ram Comal Sen, the 'native' manager of Hunter's Press, later on became the 'native' Secretary of the Asiatic Society itself. In 1846, two years after Ram comal Sen's death, Rajendralala Mitra, then a young man, joined the Asiatic Society as its Assistant Librarian. The Indian Renaissance was made possible and in fact was accelerated by the quiet but far-reaching work going on at the corner of Park Street despite all odds and adverse circumstances.

In 1808 two Committees were formed, the Physical Committee and the Library Committee, the former for the promotion of Natural History, Medicine, Physics etc. and the latter for that of Literature, Philosophy, History, Antiquities etc. William Carey, J. Leyden, A. Lockett and W. Hunter were included in both the Committees. Both these Committees went moribund in no time and the Physical Committee had to be revived in 1818 by a resolution. A new chapter of the Society opened when in 1829 its membership was made open to native Indians. Ram Comal Sen, one of the earliest Indian members of the Society and a close friend of Wilson, the then Secretary, recalled his twenty nine years with the Society when he accepted the post of native Secretary, and Wilson appointed Ram comal

to his new post only seven days before the Special Meeting of the Society in which he announced his departure for England. At this Special Meeting held on 19 December 1833 the President of the Society, Sir Edward Ryan spoke highly of the services rendered by Wilson to the Society.

In 1837, only four years after Wilson's departure, James Prinsep, the new Secretary of the Society, deciphered the Brahmi Script and was able to read the Asokan Edicts. It was a world event that revolutionised all future Oriental studies and contributed to the growth of Comparative Philology.

The Transactions of the Asiatic Society were first published under the title of Asiatick Researches in 1788, the subsequent four volumes being published in 1790, 1793, 1795 and 1797 respectively. At first the publication was private, undertaken by Manual Cantopher on the condi- tion that each member of the Society would purchase one volume at a price of Rs. 20. Later on, the Society itself undertook the responsibility of the publication. The publication Asiatick Researches was so much in demand in the literary and scholarly world that a pirated edition of the first volume came into circulation in England in 1798, and some of the volumes of the Asiatick Researches were translated into German as well as in French. Through its published Transactions the Society now came in touch with several distinguished scholarly Associations abroad such as the American Philosophical Society of Philadelphia, the Linnean Society of London, the Royal Society of Edinburgh, and the Society of Antiquities of England.

The Society also proved to be a pivotal centre of Oriental studies and research and extended its helping hand to the other two major centres of activity that paved the way to the Indian Renaissance, namely, the College at Fort William and the Serampore Mission of William Carey. In 1805 a proposal came to the Asiatic Society from the Serampore Mission to publish classical Sanskrit works with their English translations, and the first book chosen for this was the Sanskrit epic, Ramayana. For

this purpose the Society spent from its fund five thousand and five hundred rupees. From 1788 till its cessation in 1839 the journal Asiatick Researches ran into twenty volumes and was superseded by the Journal of the Asiatic Society, henceforth the official organ of the Society. The Society also started in 1905 a new serial entitled the Memoirs which was discontinued in 1933. The nucleus of the Society's own library was formed soon after the building was completed in 1808. The Fort William College which was helped a lot academically by the Society, presented books to the Society from its own collection, and another valuable collection of books came from the Palace Library of Tipu Sultan in 1808.

It may be mentioned that two decades before Ram Mohan Roy's first tract on Sati it was H. T. Colebrooke who proved from the early texts that the practice of Sati was a gross deviation from the authentic tradition. The founding fathers of the Asiatic Society were responsible for the rediscovery of India and her past.

Sir Charles Wilkins (1750-1 833) translated the Bhagavadgita into English in 1785, deciphered a number of Sanskrit inscriptions published a translation of Hitopadesa (1787) and a Grammar of the Sanskrit Language. Sir William Jones translated Kalidasa's **Sakuntala** (1789), Jayadeva's Gitagovinda (1789) and Manusamhita (1794), and edited Ritusamhara (1792). Jones also translated a Persian work Laila Majnu. The works initiated by Wilkins and Jones were continued by Colebrooke (1765-1837) and Wilson (1784-1860). Colebrooke was the President of the Society from 1806 to 1815 and contributed nineteen papers to the Transactions of the Society. He published an English translation of Jagannath Tarkapanchanan's celebrated work on Hindu law, the Vivadabhangarnava under the title Digest of Hindu Law on Contracts and Successions (1798). He also published a critical edition of the Sanskrit lexicon Amarakosha (1808). Wilson was Secretary to the Asiatic Society from 1811 to 1833 and published Kalidasa's Meghaduta (1813) and got the

eighteen principal Puranas also translated into English. He also published an edition of Kalhana's Rajatarangini (1825). Sir John Shore (1751-1834) who succeeded William Jones as President of the Society in 1794, published from a Persian version an abridged English transalation of the Yoga Vasistha and contributed six papers to the Asiatick Researches.

Most of the works of the Society are research-based and research-oriented, and have not been loudly spectacular. But its publication, the **Bibliotheca Indica**, consisting of a series of several hundred Oriental texts in Sanskrit, Arabic, Persian, Bengali, Tibetan and other Asian languages, both in original and translation, has earned the Society a rare reputation among scholars all over the world. Its Monographs were supplemented by several new series such as Public Lectures, Monthly Bulletins, Seminar Proceedings, Memorial Lectures and Memoirs (1905-33). These are in addition to the Society's Journal, Journal of the Asiatic Society, formerly, Asiatick Researches (1788-1849), Journal of the Asiatic Society of Bengal (1832-1904), Proceedings of the Asiatic Society (1865-1904), Journal and the Proceedings of the Asiatic Society (1905-1934), Journal of the Asiatic Society of Bengal (1935-1952) and Journal of the Asiatic Society (since 1953). A cursory glance at the contents of the **publications of the Asiatic Society** will show how great many historical Monographs and Oriental studies, all fruits of original research, were brought out in them. Archaeological and Geological surveys, census reports, treatises on law and revenue systems, all these prepared the solid basis for all future researches on Asia and the Orient.

Library of the Society

The Library of the Society is the grand stay, glory and honour of the Society. Its importance lies not in numerical strength but in its rich and unique contents. The collection has been built up mainly with gifts received from the members, dating back to 25 March 1784, when the Society received with thanks seven Persian manuscripts from Henri Richardson. The next gift

came from William Marsden, F.R.S., his book, History of Island of Sumatra (1783) on 10 November, 1984. Since the foundation of the Society, books, manuscripts, drawings, coins, antiquarian and other objects of historical importance were exhibited to the Society's meetings, and kept in the custody of the Secretary. As the Society had no habitat of its own, the risk of loss was serious. After the demise of the founder, the question of a permanent house for the Society was strongly felt for transacting its academic activities and for keeping and preserving for the posterity books, records, art, antiquarian and museum objects. The Society moved into its own building in the early part of 1808 and the Library was thrown open to the members and the public in the same year. Thus the Society laid the foundation of the first Academic as well as Public Library in India. The books that had been received till then formed the nucleus of the collection. Since then, gifts were pouring in from heads of States (e.g. Emperor of Russia), Institutions, Societies and individuals. Robert Home who was for some time Secretary of the Society and the first Library-in-Charge (1804), donated his small but very valuable collection of works on Art. The first accession of importance was a gift from the Seringapatam Committee (3 February 1808) being a selection from the palace library of Tipoo Sultan. The Collection contains many old and rare works. Special mention may be made of an illuminated manuscript of the Quran an old text of Gulistan, and manuscripts of Padshanamah bearing an autograph of Emperor Shahjahan. Similarly, Surveyor-General Colonel Mackenzie's collection of manuscripts and drawings were recived in December 1822.

Collections of the Library

The collection has been grouped into three Departments; e.g.

(1) Printed Books and Periodicals

(2) Manuscripts and Archives and

(3) Museum Objects.

The Printed Books Depatment has four sections, including European, Indian, Perso-Arabic, Urdu and Sino-Tibetan and South-Asian Departments

Printed books are in almost all the languages of the world and number more than 1,00,000 volumes, particularly rich in works on Indology and Asiatic lore, and in standard philological and scientific serials. The printed books in this department range in date from the latter half of the fifteenth century A.D. and one of its special features consists in the many items of rare works, otherwise unavailable, or scarcely available, including books printed in India in the late 18th and early 19th centuries.

Books

On the abolition of the College at Fort William, a much larger collection of historical and other works relating to India, the whole of its Sanskrit, Arabic, Persian, and Urdu works, mostly in manuscript, were placed under the custody of the Society, subject only to two conditions, namely, safe and careful preservation, and unrestricted accessibility to the public at all reasonable hours. Exchanges of publications were also made with institutions and learned Societies. Duplicates in the Library were exchanged with books in possession of private individuals, and members retiring from India sometimes presented or sold selections of their libraries to the Society. A collection of some illustrated works on Botany was received from Dr. N. Wallich in June 1817, which was subsequently sent to the East India Company's Botanical Gardens at Sibpur.

Acquisition by purchase has always been very insignificant. The Society's supplier in the days of Willian Jones was Peter Elmsly of London. Since 1806, the Society appointed agents in England from among its members who offered gratuitous service (e.g. Dr. Francis Gladwin, H. T. Colebrooke, Dr. H. H. Wilson and others) to select, purchase and forward all important books of Science and Oriental literature together with the leading scientific and other periodicals published in Europe.

In the 20th century Dr. N. Annandale, Dr. B. C. Law (on Buddhism), Dr. C. W. Gurner (on Greek and Latin Literature), R. P. Chanda (on Indian History and Culture), C. R. Cama (on Indo-Muslim literature and history), Bengal Club (on European History and Politics) and Dr. Pratap Chadra Chunder Literature (Nirmal Chandra Chunder's Library) and many others made gifts of large and special collections. Ananda Bazar Patrika presented a very valuable collection of about 12,000 volumes to the memory of Prafulla Chandra Sarkar. Among the institutions of foreign countries, which donated a large number of books to the Society's Library mention should be made of the Smithsonian Institute of America, Institut Danois des Exchanges, and Japan Foundation. Prof. Nirmal Kumar Bose bequeathed his library to the Society. This filled in many gaps in the collection of the Society. Jnananjan Niyogi's collection of books now forms a part of the Library. Space does not permit to record the names of other distinguished donors.

Collection of Periodicals

The periodical collection of the Society is unique in Asia, especially in its holdings of learned journals from all over the world. Even the journals of the Societies established long before the foundation of the Asiatic Society are available here. Most of these have been acquired by way of gift or by exchange with Society's publications which were, and are still, held in high esteem by the learned world. Of course, its collection in Asian languages is comparatively weak. Nevertheless, there are some unique journals in Indian languages which are not available elsewhere. There are about 5,000 titles of learned journals of which about 100 titles only are subscribed and these run into 1,12,000 volumes or thereabout. Scholars from all parts of India and abroad visit this library for consultations of this unique collection.

Rare Book Division

In 1978 the Council decided to open a Rare Book Division.

The preliminary screening of the collection has since been started. Among the earliest printed books mention may be made of the following: Julii Firmici Astronomicorum libri octo integri (Venice 1499), Kitabal-Qanum (Arabic/Romae 1595), Kripar Sastrer Arthabhed (Bengali in Roman Character, Lisbon 1743); S. Purchas's Purchas : His Pilgrimage (London, 1 61 4), N. Halhed's Grammar of the Bengal Language, (Hooghly, 1778), Malabar and English Dictionary, (Madras, 1779), Rasamanjari (Sanskrit, Banaras, 1791), Ram Ram Bose's Lipimala (Bengali. Serampore, 1802), The Ramayana 3 vols, (Bengali, Serampore, 1803), Hitopadesa (Sanskrit, Serampore, 1804), Colebrooke's Grammar of the Sanskrit language Vol.1 (Serampore, 1805).

Library Organisation

Robert Home, the artist, volunteered his services to look after the Library in the early days and was in fact the first unofficial Librarian. When the Library-cum-Museum building was erected, the question of appointment of staff for maintenance came up. In 1808 it was decided to appoint a Librarian for the management of the Library. Mr.W.L.Gibbons was appointed the first regular Librarian to work under the direction and control of the Society. He was followed by Alexander Csoma de koros (1833), Heramba Nath Thakor (Assistant Librarian 1833), Dr. L. Burlini, Kissori Chand Mitra (1846), Dr. Edward Roer (1843), Raja Rajendraial Mitra (1847), Gaurdas Bysack (1856), Lalgopal Datta (1865). Kristodhar Datta (Acting, 1865), Pratap Chandra Ghosh (1868), Balai Dutta, Sarasi Kumar Saraswati and others. The Librarian used to hold concurrently the post of the Assistant Secretary of the Society. With the passage of time the popularity of the Library increased and the authorities felt the need for framing regulations for the management of the Library. The new regulations came into force in January 1820 and were subsequently revised a number of times according to the need. The Society possesses a magnificent library. It has many rare and valuable mansucripts and books. The first inventory of this collection was made in 1833. The Society then possessed only

about 1000 volumes each in the European and Oriental sections. In 1925 there were about 50,000 volumes of books and manuscripts.

Now, there are about 2,50,000 volumes of books, periodicals, pamphlets, manuscripts, xylographs, besides works of art, coins and copper plates, sculptures, rock edict and other antiquarian objects. In his presidential address in 1925 Sir R. N. Mookherji said: "It is not the number of volumes in the Library but the worth of the collection to scholars in prosecution of research which makes the value of the Library and we can confidently say that no other library, at any rate in Asia, contains as rich a store of Eastern knowledge and learning as the Asiatic Society Library. Since the establishment of the Library much has been done and is being done, in spite of financial handicaps, to improve conditions and to enrich collections, so as to render Society's unique Library of greater utility to all members and inquisitive readers. In spite of best efforts, the Library is deficient in many ways. There are many basic books, especially in modern Indian and other Asian Languages, that the Society ought to have, but having no means to buy them, cannot acquire. To obviate these difficulties and to keep the Centre of Research current with all materials, the Society decided in 1 927, at the instance of the then Treasurer Dr. S. L. Hora, to create a permanent Library Endowment Fund to which a sum of approximately three thousand rupees was subscribed by members of the Council for Library purposes alone, and an appeal had been issued to the general body of members for liberal donations. In addition, the Council realised from the early days that to bring the scholars and the books together there should be catalogues of the collection of books and manuscripts and they undertook compilation and publication of catalogues of books, manuscripts, periodicals, curiosities and bibliographies, which still continue.

The Society made its first modest attempt to publish a catalogue of its collection, in 1833, for the books in European Languages only, edited by L. Burline, followed by the catalogues

prepared by E. Roer (1843). R. L. Mitra (1856), Walter Arnold Sion (1884), H. B. Perie (1910) and others, and the last catalogue was published in 1934. Publication of short catalogues for books in Asian Languages is now in progress. So far catalogues of Arabic and Persian books prepared by Muliar Rahman in 1958-1967, Hindi books by G. N. Bhattacharji in 1967, and Bengali books by S. Chaudhuri in 1968, have been published. The Bengali catalogue includes an index to articles of most of the Bengali periodicals in the Library of the Society. Kemp's Catalogue of scientific periodicals available in Calcutta Libraries(1918) is invaluable. The time has come now for making a new catalogue of the entire collection according to subjects. The Reading Room of the Society is on the first floor of the new building. The Library is kept open on week days.The Library is organised into four sections:

Manuscripts Collection

The Asiatic Society holds rare and invariable collection. It is varied and rich, and covers most of the Indian languages and scripts and even several Asian ones, e.g., Assamese, Bengali, Gujarati, Gurumukhi, Kanarese, Urdu, Marathi, Modi, Nagari, Newari, Oriya, Rajasthani, Sarada, Armenian, Sinhalese, Arabic, Persian, Pushto, Javanese, Turki, Burmese, Chinese, Siamese, Tibetan etc. The materials used for the manuscripts are also varied: palm and palmyra leaves, barks of different trees, papers of various grades.

The four sections devoted to the manuscripts are as under:

(a) Sanskritic Section : This Section comprises of manuscripts in Sanskrit and Modern Indian Languages, which range in date from the 7th Century A.D. and number about thirty thousand. Rich and varied in textual contents the collection is an epitome of India's achievements in diverse spheres of life and learning. Some of the manuscripts have fine miniature illustrations, the earliest of which belongs to the 10th Century A.D.

(b) Islamic Section : This Section comprises of manuscripts in Arabic, Persian, Turkish, Pushto, Urdu, etc. numbering more than seven thousand, ranging in date from the first quarter of the 12th Century A.D. Some of the manuscripts belonged to the Mughal Imperial Library, Tipu Sultan's Library and Fort William College Library. Some are extremely rare and some are rich and varied in textual contents. They cover every branch of Islamic history and learning. In some, the calligraphy is most excellent while a few others bear miniature paintings of high quality and style, some of them being autographed.

(c) Sino-Tibetan and South-East Asian Section : This Section comprises of manuscripts and Xylographs in Burmese, Chinese, Tibetan, Siamese etc. Chinese manuscripts relate to Chinese translations of the Indian Buddhist texts, while the Tibetan group includes the entire set of the Kangyur and the Bstangyur, besides also individual Xylographs and manuscripts. Manuscript works in Burmese, Siamese, Javanese, etc. are interesting for studies in the history and culture of these countries and also for study of Buddhism.

(d) English Section : This Section comprises a few English manuscripts in the Society. These are from Nathaniel Halhed, James Prinsep, Buchanan Hamilton, Alexander Csoma de koros and others.

Sanskrit

The manuscripts cover the period from 7th c. A.D. down to the 19th century. These are useful source materials to illustrate the development of the Indian scripts (especially Bengali, Nagari etc.). The colophons and post-colophons contain information relating to socio-economic conditions of the people. Besides, they help us to fix the chronology of the Royal dynasties of India. Where the inscriptions fail to ascertain dates and chronology, the manuscripts may throw some light, provided a thorough critical study of these and their colophons and postcolophons were made.

Some of the rare Sanskrit manuscripts may be mentioned here. Brihati (from Kavindracharya's collection), Amrita Vindu (11th c.), Kiranavali, Charucharya, Nartaka Nirnaya, Parasika-prakasa, Sanskrita-ratnakara, Lalitavistara, Horoscope of a muslim of the Mughal Court (1640 A.D.) A Deed of Mortgage (1639), Ramayana (Bengali) of Ramananda Yati, Vajrayana text (11th c.), a text on Buddhist Nyaya, Rigveda Padapatha, Laghu-Kalachakra-tika, Kalachakravetara, Kuttanimatam, Vajravalinama mannadalopayika, Ramacharita of Sandhyakar Nandi, Bhattikavyatika of Srinivasa, and Paragali Mahabharata.

The manuscript of Kubjikamatam is of the 7th Century A.D. The manuscript of Rigveda Padapatha, copied in 1362 A.D., is perhaps "the oldest manuscript of the Rigveda."

Islamic

Of the many Islamic Manuscripts there are some which are extremely rare and unique. Of these only a few may be mentioned: Tahdhib Sharh As-Sab' at Mullaqat (early 12th c. Arabic), Qalaid al-Iquian wa Mahasin al-Ayan (12th c.), Kharidat al-Qasr (12th c.), Al-Jam Baynas as-Sahihin abridged version with autograph, (13th c.), A-Madkhul(13th c.), Tafsir-i-Quran (Persian, 13th c., important also for calligraphy), Tuhfat al-Ahbar fi usul at Hadith wa'l Akhbar (15th c.), Kitab al-I'lan (18th c.), Saha' if-i-Shara' if or Duraral Mansur (Persian, 19th c., an autographed copy), and Adab-i-Alamgiri (18th c.).

Illustrated Manuscripts

There are large numbers of illuminated and illustrated manuscripts of different schools, many of which are unique for their calligraphy, delicacy of their lines, and elegance of composition and charming colour schemes. These miniatures still afford glimpses of India's past achievements, Of these unique manuscripts (earliest belonging to the 10th Century A.D.) mention may be made of a few: Astasahasrika Prajnaparamita, Aparimitayurnama Mahayana sutra, Pancharaksha, Paramarthanama Sangati, Devimahatmya. Viveka Panchamrita.

Bhagavatgita, Shahnama, Kullayat-i-Saadi, Suwaru'l aqalim, Farang-i-Aurang Shahi, Ain-i-Akbari, Diwan-i-Makhfi, Qissa-i-Nush-Afarin, Jamiut-Twarikh, Amir nama Tutinama, Iyar-i-Danesh, Bihar-i-Danesh, Tarjuma Mahabharata, Tafribul-Imarah (by Silchand, dedicated to J. H. Lushington), and Imaratut-Akbar (by Chitarmal for James Duncan).

Many scholars are using the collection for editing their texts and for translation in modern languages.

Archives/English Manuscripts

In the Library there are preserved a large number of old letters some of which date back to1784, just after the Society was founded. These letters were received by the Society from persons belonging to different walks of life, requesting information on such subjects as old and rare manuscripts, ancient monuments, coins etc. Some among the writers of these letters were persons well known for their literary, scientific and other cultural accomplishments. These old files constitute important documents relating to the history of the Society, as also of many other scientific and humanistic organisations that were established in India either in the 19th or in the 20th century.

Other Collections

Urdu

The Society has a fine collection of about 234 Urdu manuscripts many of which were received as a gift from the Fort William College (founded in 1800), Fort William College decided to award prizes, at the instance of J. S. Gilchrist, for standard original and translated works in the Hindusthani language, produced in the College.

Sino-Tibetan and Burmese

The Society has a complete set of Kanjur and Tanjur texts of the Buddhist scriptures and some extra-canonical works. These were collected by B. H. Hodgson and A. Csoma de koros. A section of the collection has been catalogued. There are over one

hundred titles of Chinese books, some of which are rare and valuable for Chinese studies. These cover almost all the subjects relating to Chinese Culture, Civilization and Science and Buddhism. Subjects covered include Classical Literature, Language. History, Geography, Topography, Philosophy, Religion, manners and customs, biography of scholars, sciences (Botanical, Astronimical, Zoological).

Bengali Manuscripts

Other than Sanskrit, a few Bengali manuscripts have been found written by Bengali Brahmins residing in Varanasi. Parageli Mahabharat, Chuti Khan'sAsvamedha Parva, and many other important manuscripts were purchased. Mss. donated by Justice Ramaprosad Mukherjee and Sri A Roy enriched the collection. Now we have 703 Bengali Mss. and 12 Assamese manuscripts in the collection of the Asiatic Society. It comprises Asiatic Society's own collection, Government collection, Indian Museum collection and donors' collection. At present, the collection of Bengali manuscripts in the possession of Asiatic Society is rich in respect of number and rarity. The Society has manuscripts on Ramayana, Mahabharata, Srimadbhagavat, Mangala Kavyas, treatises on Vaisnava faith and its allied subjects. Folk literature, erotic verses and Vaisnaba Sahajiya Cult etc.

Rajasthani

The Society possesses very rare, valuable and important Raiasthani Manuscripts which date the pre-middle and middle years. Under the guidance of Dr. Sukumar Sen, the Society prepared and brought out a descriptive catalogue, Part 1, of the same in 1957.

Except a few short treatises on genealogies of Rajput warriors or Jain monks, the bulk belongs to eulogistic literature known as Prashasti Kavya. A few manuscripts are on traditional and Puranic themes, such as the story of the Goddess Karani, Krishna and Rukmini, Rama and Siva. Of special interest are the romances unique to Rajasthan and its literaure. The best known amongst them is the story of Dhola and Maru. There are other manuscripts which throw ample light on the rulers of Rajasthan.

2

INDIRA GANDHI NATIONAL CENTRE FOR THE ARTS LIBRARY, NEW DELHI

The Indira Gandhi National Centre for the Arts (IGNCA) was established in the memory of Smt. Indira Gandhi, the prime minster of India. It is visualized as a centre encompassing the study and experience of all the arts — each form with its own integrity, yet within a dimension of mutual interdependence, interrelated with nature, social structure and cosmology.

This view of the arts, integrated with, and essential to the larger matrix of human culture, is predicated upon Smt. Gandhi's recognition of the role of the arts as essential to the integral quality of person, at home with himself and society. It partakes of the holistic worldview so powerfully articulated throughout Indian tradition, and emphasized by modern Indian leaders from Mahatma Gandhi to Rabindranath Tagore.

The arts are here understood to comprise the fields of creative and critical literature, written and oral; the visual arts, ranging from architecture, sculpture, painting and graphics to general material culture, photography and film; the performing arts of music, dance and theatre in their broadest connotation; and all else in fairs, festivals and lifestyle that has an artistic dimension. In its initial stages the Centre will focus attention on India; it will later expand its horizons to other civilizations and cultures. Through diverse programmes of research, publication, training, creative activities and performance, the IGNCA seeks to place the arts within the context of the natural and human environment. The fundamental approach of the Centre is all its work will be both multidisciplinary and interdisciplinary.

Recognizing the need to encompass and preserve the distributed fragments of Indian art and culture, a pioneering attempt has been made by Indira Gandhi National Centre for the Arts (IGNCA) to serve as a major resource centre for the arts, especially written, oral and visual materials. One of the programmes of this centre, in collaboration with UNDP, is to utilize multimedia computer technology to create a wide variety of software packages that communicate cultural information. Multimedia technology allows the user to interact and explore the subject in a non-linear mode by combining audio, text, graphics, animation and video on a computer.

Collections

The IGNCA is a National Information System and a Data Bank of the arts, humanities, cultural heritage with a fully supported reference library of multimedia collections. This information System and Data Bank will serve as a major resource centre for research in humanities, in the arts, in the disciplines of Archaeology, Anthropology, History, Philosophy, Literature, Language, Arts , Crafts etc. It is proposed to have very large library of microfilms / microfisches along with the printed material on Greater India, South Asia, Southeast, Asia and West Asia. Language won't be a barrier in its collection development policy. It is also proposed to have a collection of about half a million works during the next few years.

The reference library of IGNCA has a large collection of primary and secondary material in the broad areas of humanities and the arts. It constitutes books, reprographics of several folios of unpublished Sanskrit, Pali, Persian and Arabic manuscripts in microfilm and microfische, Photographs and slides. The Collection includes books on archaeology, philosophy, religion and ritual studies, history and anthropology, art and literature as well as folk, pastoral and community studies. The library is enriched by many rare collections of illustrious scholars who have made path-breaking contributions in fields related to arts. The library concentrates on encyclopaedias, dictionaries,

bibliographies, atlases and catalogues of unpublished manuscripts of Indian and Asian origin. Its holdings and expertize are complemented by those of the other divisions of the Centre.

Rare Books

Acquisition of rare books is a special feature of the Library. It has acquired books published in 18th and 19th centuries such as: The Travels of Sir John Charlin (1688); The Ceremonies and Religious Customs of various Nations of the known world together with historical annotations/Bernard Picard (1733-37); The works of Sir William Jones,(1759-1801); Considerations of Indian Affairs/William Botts.(1772); Journal of a route to Nagpore (1790); Narrative of the Compaign in India/Dirom (1793); Oriental Repertory (1793-94);A Journey from Bengal to England through the northern part of India Kashmire, Afghanistan/George Forester (1797);Oriental Memories/James Forbes (1831); A Sketch of the History of the East India Company from its first formation to the passing/Robert Grant, (1813); Letters Written in a Mahratta Camp/Thomas Duer Broughton (1815); Views in the Himalayan Mountains /James Baille Fraser (1820); The History of Jawa/T.S. Raffles (1817); An Account of the fishes found in river Ganges/Francis hamilton (1822); Historical Fragments of the Moghul Empire of the Mora-Hoes and of the English Concerns in Hindustan from the year/ Robert Orme (1825); The History of British India/James Mills(1826);

Personal Collections

A Unique feature of the library is the Personal Collection of eminent scholars and artists. Already major Collection have been gifted to the library. These Include:

Dr. Suniti Kumar Chatterjee Collection - Suniti Kumar Chatterjee (1890-1977) belonged to a generation of intellectuals who gave Indian thought a new direction. A multidisciplinary scholar, philologist and connoisseur of art, Chatterjee was professor of linguistics and languages at the University of Calcutta for thirty years.

Dr. Thakur Jaideva Singh Collection - Thakur Jaideva Singh (1893-1986) was a versatile genius and a rare combination of a philosopher, Sanskritist and musicologist and leading expert on Kashmir Saivaism.

Krishna Kriplani Collection - Krishna Kriplani was a close associate of Gurudev Rabindranath Tagore and later secretary to Maulana Azad.

Acharya Hazari Prasad Dwivedi Collection - Acharya Hazari Prasad Dwivedi (1907-1979) was a man off phenomenal reading and an encyclopaedic mind. He was a doyen among teachers and a well-known Hindi scholar.

Heeramaneck Collection - The rich collection of Nasi Heeramaneck, comprising about 2,500 books, was donated by his wife Alice Heeramanech. The collection contains several books on Asian arts. The rich collection of Nasi Heeramaneck, comprising about 2,500 books, was donated by his wife Alice Heeramanech. The collection contains several books on Asian arts. The rich collection of Nasi Heeramaneck, comprising about 2,500 books, was donated by his wife Alice Heeramanech. The collection contains several books on Asian arts.

Lance Dane Collection - A significant contribution of about 5,000 rare books, covering Indian art and architecture, has been made by this renowned photographer.

Chaturvedi Dwarka Prasad Collection - More than 12,000 books and 2,500 periodicals from the library of Chaturvedi Dwarka Prasad Sharma have been acquired through his grandson Shail Nath Chaturvedi. The illustrious scholar was an authority on modern Indian history.

Area Collections

Research and exchange programmes with South-East Asia, East Asia and Eurasia have brought in cultural material and acquisitions, covering a wide range of disciplines, enriching the core collections on the region

Series and Catalogue

The library is concentrating on building a complete corpus of printed material on Catalogue of manuscripts of indic and Asian origin published in all parts of the world. So for besides the Catalogues Catalogrum, it has acquired catalogues of major Sanskrit, Persian, Arabic manuscripts from libraries/research institutions of India, UK, USA, FRG, GDR, France, Italy and Japan.The series acquisition programme includes the LD series; Ecolede France; Institute of Indian Studies, Pondicherry Series; K. P. Jayaswal Research Institute, Patna; Satapitaka series, Bibliotheca Indica, Chowkhambha Series; Gaekwad Oriental Series, Barodal ; Pali Text Society Series; Rajasthan Puratana Granthmala; Sampurnanand Sanskrit Vishvavidyalaya Granthmala; Sri Ananthacharya Indological Research Institute Series; Woolner Indological Series, and many others.

Journals

The library subscribes to over 400 journals relating to arts. It is also building a serial collection of back volumes of periodicals. Among the journals obtained are Central Asian Survey, Asian Theatre Journal, Asian Music, Dance Chronicle,Australian Aboriginal Studies, SPAFA Journal, South East Asian Review, Russian Studies in History, Journal of the Oriental Institute, Praehistorische Zietschouft, MankindQuarterly, Journal of American Oriental Sociology, Journal of Ritual Studies, Leonardo, Visual Computer, Visual Anthropology, Journal of the History of Ideas, Revive de L'Art,Artibus Asiae, and Journal of American Oriental Society.

Microfilms/Microfische

A unique feature of the IGNCA library is the reprographic compilation of unpublished manuscripts in Indian and foreign collections from private and public libraries. A pioneering attempt has been made to bring under one roof primary sources of the Indian tradition lying scattered, fragmented, inaccessible or worse, in danger of extinction. At present the library contains

about ten million folios of unpublished Sanskrit, Pali, Persian and Arabic manuscripts.

Reprographic material of various primary and secondary texts has been obtained from many foreign institutions including Bibliotheque Nationale (Paris), Cambridge University Library (Cambridge, UK), Staatsbibliothek (Berlin), INION (Russia), Wellcome Institute for the History of Medicine (London), and Oriental & India Office Collection, British Library (London).

Manuscripts are acquired in the form of micrographic records from major institutions across the country, like Khuda Baksh Oriental Public Library (Patna), Bhandarkar Oriental Research Institute (Pune), Asiatic Society (Calcutta), Manipur State Kala Academy (Imphal), Atombapu Research Centre (Imphal), Vaidika Samsodhana Mandala (Pune), Saraswati Bhawan Library (Varanasi), Government Oriental MSS Library (Madras), Oriental Research Institute and MSS Library (Trivandrum), Shri Ram Verma Government Sanskrit College (Tripunithura), Tanjavur Maharaja Serfoji's Saraswati Mahal Library (Tanjavur), and Shri Ranbir Sanskrit Research Institute (Jammu).

Visual Library

A photograph-and-slide collection is being developed. Slide collections of over one lakh art objects and illustrated miniatures in Indian and foreign collections have been compiled and documented. These include slide collections from the victoria and Albert Museum, Chester Beatty Collection through courtesy of Indian National Trust for Art and Culture Heritage (INTACH), American Committee for South Asian Art (ACSAA), British Museum, and Oriental and India Office Collection, British

Information and Databank

IGNCA has been designated as the nodal agency for all matters relating to art, humanities and cultural heritage by the Government of India. It is to provide computerized storage,

retrieval and dissemination of information on all aspects of arts and cultural heritage

In its ambitious endeavour to preserve in various forms the vast cultural heritage and make it accessible for research and dissemination, the Centre has launched an extensive computerization programme to maintain, analyze and develop multi-media databases and information systems. Special efforts are made to network programmes with various institutions inside and outside the country. A global computer network of all cultural institutions with IGNCA as the nodal agency is also being envisaged.

Cultural Archive

Material relating to different genres in the original and in the other forms of copies is collected, classified and catalogued in the cultural archives of the Centre. The archives are enriched by personal collection, ethnographic collections documentation and cultural exchange.

Many scholars, artists and art enthusiasts, over the last decades, have carefully and dedicatedly collected materials of their interest ranging from literature and personal histories, recitation, painting, music to folklore and tribal arts. Some of these rare collections of ethnography and audio/visual documentation of old masters and rare art forms have been acquired by the archives.

Ethnographic collections constitute core collections consisting of originals, reproductions and reprographic formats used as basic resource material in the projects of lifestyle studies. In-house documentation includes video and film documentations of various events of the Centre. Emphasis is also given to researched audio and video documentation in various studies sponsored by the Centre. A major collection of the archives comprise cultural material obtained through cultural exchange and research in area studies. The archival collections are

conserved, documented and made available for the purposes of research and dissemination.

Literature

This category consists of information, archival material in literature of various languages. A noted collection is of R. C. Rangra.

Dr. R. C. Rangra has interviewed over 90 Indian writers, in the different languages of the country. The interviews are not mere biographical sketches of the authors, but are in-depth discussions about their literary works. The audio tapes are also accompanied by transcriptions of the interviews with annotations by the authors themselves.

Architechture and Sculpture

Under this category IGNCA has the Lance Dane Collection of Photo Archives of Art comprising 1,00,000 B/W negatives and color transparencies on the Art and Architecture of India, Nepal and Combodia. This collection also has about 1,000 Sculptures figurings and artefacts, and wall rubbings of Angkor Wat.

The Shambunath Mitra collection has over 9,000 B/W negatives, detailed photo index cards and gazetteers of the Bengal terracotta temples of Bishnupur, Bankura, Burdwan, Hooghly, Howrah and Midnapur Districts.

Photographs

In this section, several prestigious collections have been acquired. The most notable of these are the glass-plate negatives and original prints of Raja Deen Dayal, the Grandmaster of Indian Photography. Another prestigious collection is that of Henri Cartier Bresson's photographs of India comprising candid shots of the Indian freedom struggle. D. R. D. Wadia collection and photographs of the noted Photo-historian Sunil Janah, known for his rural life and freedom struggle pictures.

Raja Lala Deen Dayal Collection

Raja Lala Deen Dayal was the premiere pioneer in Indian photography. He was a great artist and a technician, and hence his legacy of negative plates and original prints are of great importance to the world of photography. His Collection comprises over 2700 glass plate negatives, 200 original prints and other material such as exhibition prints, registers and photographic equipment.

Henri Cariter-Bresson Collection

Mr. Henri Cariter-Bresson is one of the world's greatest photographers who, during his visit to India recorded for posterity the visuals of the birth of a nation. Mr. Cartier-Bresson shot candid moments of the freedom struggle in India as a pioneer of 'Concerned Photographer's Movement'. From the Cartier-Bresson Collection 107 photographs are being acquired by the Archives.

D. R. D. Wadia Collection

The D. R. D. Wadia collection comprising photographs of political leaders, scientists, diplomats, dancers and landscapes.

Sunil Janah Collection

Sunil Janah is a distinguished photo-journalist whose works cover Indian History, especially during the struggle for freedom and the subsequent period. The Collection also contains profiles of the people of India — statesmen, city and rural / tribal dwellers as also the many facets of indian life — the arts, agriculture and industry.

Manuscripts Collection

A National Mission has been launched to locate, enumerate, preserve and catalogue Indian manuscripts within the country and abroad with a view to enhancing their access and conserving them for posterity.A National Manuscripts Library is to be set up in Indira Gandhi National Centre for the Arts, New Delhi as a part of the Mission's activities. The Library is to be the central

repository for original and microfilmed copies of all Indian manuscripts.Under the National Mission, manuscripts will be documented and preserved by adopting a multi-pronged strategy which include spreading public awareness, surveys on extending need-based infrastructural support to the major custodial institutions, conservation, micro-filming, digitisation and cataloguing. A National Empowered Committee under the chairmanship of the Minister-in-charge of Culture and the Executive Committee under the chairmanship of Secretary (Culture) have been constituted to provide policy advice, guidance, prepare action plans and evolve procedures for implementation of the objectives of the National Mission for Manuscripts.Prior to Independence, a large number of cultural objects including manuscripts had moved from the Indian sub-continent to different parts of the world. These objects are scattered among innumerable museums and private collections. There was no international covenant for the restitution of such objects.The Antiquities (Export Control) Act, was promulgated in 1947. It was succeeded by the enactment of the Antiquities and Art Treasures Act, 1972. Under this Act, illegal export of manuscripts is a crime. Moreover, registration of manuscripts is mandatory under this Act. In respect of the countries which are signatories to the UNESCO Convention on "Means of Prohibiting and Preventing the Illicit Imports, Exports and Transfer of Ownership of Cultural Property", action can be initiated as per the provisions of the Convention. India is a signatory to this Convention. The Archaeological Survey of India has been taking action wherever instances of objects taken illegally out of the country have come to its notice.

National Mission for Manuscripts

Survey to identify manuscripts, acquiring or copying and preserving them would form the most immediate tasks of the National Mission for Manuscripts, expected to be launched by early October. According to the Mission Document finalised by the Department of Culture, there is no accurate account of the

number of manuscripts available in the country. Various sources place the estimates differently. Hence, it becomes imperative to identify the manuscripts available, as they are with custodians ranging from institutions to individuals.

The manuscripts once identified have to be acquired or copied so that they can be preserved at least in the state they are in. It is this urgency that Secretary Culture, Shri N. Gopalaswami, underlined while inaugurating a one-day seminar, where the Discussion paper for the Mission Document was circulated. Quoting the words of Whiltey Stokes, Secretary to the Council of Governor General in 1868, the Secretary Culture said what was said about manuscripts in India 134 years ago was still relevant.

Mr. Stokes then writing on the state of the manuscripts had said that 'no time should be lost in taking measures to save the manuscripts which are degenerating because of the climate, white ants and declining interest.' Experts, subject scholars, government representatives and the implementing agencies participated in the seminar to consider the proposals in the Discussion Paper.

According to the Discussion Paper only a small percentage of the manuscripts has been surveyed and catalogued and their number may not be more than 20-25 per cent of the estimated total. The most daunting task for the Mission arises from the fact that the custodians of the manuscripts are dispersed and unidentified. Manuscripts are in the possession of various institutions - libraries, museums and archives, religious bodies, private collectors as also individuals. According to a conservative estimate there are over five million manuscripts in India in various forms and scripts, 60,000 in European countries and 1.5 million in South Asia and Asian countries. Sanskrit manuscripts form 67 per cent of the total number. Some of the practical difficulties anticipated are in preserving the manuscripts once they are identified. Since the manuscripts are in different forms and materials like birch bark, leather, palm leaf, paper etc. it is

necessary to train the owners of the manuscripts in their preservation.

The Mission has designated IGNCA as the Nodal Agency for implementing the Mission. The Mission has an estimated outlay of Rs. 250 million for 5 years. The implementation period will coincide with the 10th Five-Year Plan. The Directorate of the Mission will be located at the Centre and IGNCA will also set up a National Manuscripts Library.

The IGNCA Trust will constitute the National Empowered Committee for the implementation of the Mission, chaired by the President of the IGNCA Executive Committee. The Empowered Committee shall have as members the member Secretary. IGNCA, Secretary Culture, The Director General of the National Archives and 10 - 15 others nominated by IGNCA.

Opening discussions at the seminar, Prof. N.R.Shetty, Member Secretary, IGNCA, gave a short background on the work the Centre has done with regard to documenting, preserving and dissemination of the manuscript wealth of the country. He also emphasized on the need to create a National Register of manuscripts as one of the first steps in the implementation of the Mission.

A substantial number of Indian manuscripts have been taken outside the country. It will be part of the Mission's efforts to get copies of these manuscripts, for which budgetary provision has been made. The Mission will also extend financial help to institutions, universities and other sources that have considerable number of manuscripts to improve their storage facility. Some of the States where major wealth of manuscripts are available are Tamil Nadu, Uttar Pradesh, Andhra Pradesh, Rajasthan and Orissa. (See list for major State administered institutions with huge collection of manuscripts).

The Mission Document states that the objectives of the Mission are: (1) To enhance the access to the manuscripts, improve awareness about cultural inheritance and encourage the

use of manuscripts for educational and research purpose and lifelong learning; (2) to facilitate conservation and preservation of manuscripts through training, awareness and financial support; (3) to document and catalogue Indian manuscripts, wherever they may be, maintain accurate and up-to-date information about them and the conditions under which they may be consulted; (4) to promote ready access to these manuscripts through publication, both in book form as well as machine readable form; (5) to boost scholarship and research in the study of Indian languages and manuscriptology; (6) to build up a National Manuscripts Library at IGNCA.

Availability of Manuscripts in some primier institutions of the country is shown in the table below:

S. No.	Organisation	Number of Manuscripts
1.	Sampurnanand Sanskrit University, Varanasi	1,20,000
2.	Government Oriental Manuscript Library, Chennai	66,077
3.	Oriental Institute and Manuscript Library, Tiruananthapuram	56,000
4.	Saraswati Mahal Library, Thanjavur	47,000
5.	Adayar Library and Research Centre, Chennai	40,000
6.	Orissa State Museum, Bhuvaneshwar	25,000
7.	Andhra Pradesh Oriental Manuscript Library & Research Institute, Hyderabad	21,136
8.	State-Central Library, Hyderabad	17,000
9.	Rajasthan State Archives, Jaipur	14,000
10.	Rajasthan Oriental Research Institute, Jodhpur	12,262
11.	Government Manuscript Library, Allahabad	11,000

3

THE DEPARTMENT OF MANUSCRIPTOLOGY LIBRARY, INSTITUTE OF ASIAN STUDIES, CHENNAI

The Institute of Asian Studies in Chennai, is a joint venture launched by a few scholars from India and Japan and its main aim is to promote academic research on the cultural facets of Asian countries. One of its main objectives is the quest for perception of Asian literature and culture as a unified and composite whole, transcending geographical, linguistic, and cultural barriers.

Many eminent scholars from Western Europe, the former Soviet states, and the United States have made invaluable contributions to Oriental culture. Similarly, laden with emotional as well as intellectual involvement, few Asian scholars have also devoted themselves hear and soul to Asian Studies. Yet, the area of studies covered so far is not considerable and much more remains to be done. This is brought home to us by the ignorance that prevails in the world of scholarship about the similarities and diversities that exist among the Asian cultures. Only a few Asian works are available in translations in the various languages of the people of Asia. The paucity of reference material is another limitation to scholars who pursue Asiatic researches. Moreover, there are only a few centres of study which are devoted to the study of Asian cultures in depth. The Institute of Asian Studies in Chennai has been established with a view to overcoming the existing limitations and to pooling together the scattered resource persons and materials available in various countries so as to

enable our academics to carry out research on various aspects of the cultural heritage of the people of Asia in a very systematic way.

The Institute proposes to introduce the teaching of all important Asian languages and literatures sequentially. Translations of great works (literary, philosophical, theological and so forth) will also be undertaken by this Institute. Promoting comparative studies in Asian literature and of the philosophical works of Asian countries will be one of the important activities of the Institute. It is proposed to establish a strong faculty of archaeology which should engage in undertaking the much needed explorations in various parts of Asia and also serve as an up-to-date information centre of all archaeological works in Asia.

One of the main faculties of the Institute, namely the faculty of manuscriptology, is designed in such a way that its programmes include collections of all unpublished materials available on palm-leaf and other manuscripts and preserving them from further decay and disintegration. This vital part of the Institute will be engaged in protecting the cultural treasures of the people of Asia from decay and deterioration and publishing them with detailed editorial notes and critical commentaries.

Steps will be taken for the preparation of all reference materials and classification of the data available for all kinds of research on Asian culture. The Institute will collaborate with other research centres and universities of international reputation which are engaged in research on Asian culture with a view to encouraging academic research on Asian culture in a wider perspective. The Institute will embrace all modern aids to research and keep academic research in step with the development in current technology. Apart from its programmes pertaining to the preparation of reference materials, the Institute conducts language teaching programmes and Ph. D. programmes. It organizes a number of seminars, conferences, and workshops at the national as well as international level. Above all, recognizing that informed independent research scholars are the life-blood of the

various projects the Institute undertakes, it gives sound training to young scholars and helps them to work with dedication and a full sense of commitment. The Institute in short is designed as an international academic centre for cross-cultural studies and it invites scholars of good academic repute from various countries interested in Asian culture and enable them to conduct their own research on Asia languages, cultures and literatures under one roof.

This non-profit research centre was registered as an autonomous Society in 1982 and it is governed by a team of members in the capacity of the Board of Governors. Eminent personalities from various walk of life - judiciary, education, government, culture -who evince a keen interest in Asian culture, language, and literature form the Board of Governors which is headed by Justice V.R. Krishna Iyer.

The Institute plans to start separate departments for all the Asian languages in due course. At present it has nine faculties which are engaged in various academic programmes. The language faculties have the following four components namely: language instruction; translation; preparation of reference material; and comparative studies.

Language instruction is in English and it is given in three stages namely: introductory course; advanced course; and special courses in language, literature, and culture.

Translation being an important mode of cultural transmission, the Institute has a number of programmes which are designed to translate Asian classics from one language into another to enable a mutual flow of ideas from one linguistic community into another. During the initial stages literary classics with a universal perspective and relevance in the important languages in Asia are being accepted for translation.

To begin with, the reference works prepared by the Institute will be in English and the materials include encyclopedias for literatures, arts, cultures, folklore and so on of the Asian countries,

multi-lingual dictionaries, descriptive catalogues of manuscripts, an archaeological atlas, descriptive surveys of folk culture, encyclopedias of place names. Such works prepared with a wider Asian perspective will form basic source material not only for cross-cultural studies but also for the students of comparative studies and researchers in the respective individual languages.

The following nine departments have been founded so far. With the shifting of the Institute to its permanent premises in March 1996, eight more departments will be opened so that its activities will be expanded to more areas. Moreover, collaboration with a few Japanese, American, and german universities will start in the next academic year. the departments are:

Tamil Studies; Kannada Studies; Telugu Studies; Buddhism; Manuscriptology; Japanese Studies, Translation; and a Publications Division.

Languages

The Department of Tamil Studies is engaged in the preparation of reference materials in English on various aspects of the linguistic, literary, and cultural heritage of the Tamil-speaking community of South India and of the Tamils spread all over the world. One of the main projects of this department is an Encyclopedia of Tamil Literature in about 10 volumes. The Institute has already published the first three volumes of this important work. In addition to this, this department is engaged in the preparation of teaching materials which will assist foreign scholars to learn the Tamil language in a systematic way. It is also engaged in the preparation of concordances to few Tamil texts. The department of Tamil Studies offers courses in Tamil language both at the introductory and advanced levels. It has exchange programmes with several universities in addition to a PhD programmes in which a number of scholars are working on certain aspects on tamil literature and culture. This department is funded mainly by the government of Tamil Nadu.

The department of Kannada studies is engaged in the

preparation of a multi-volume Multi-lingual Dictionary of Kannada-Tamil-English-Japanese. The first volume of this work has already come out and the remaining three volumes are expected to be released in the foreseeable future.

The department of Telugu Studies is engaged in the preparation of a five-volume History of Telugu Literature and a six-volume Encyclopedia of the Telugu Literature in English. In addition, the department is conducting teaching programmes similar to that of the department of Kannada Studies and it is engaged in several projects pertaining to palm-leaf manuscripts.

The department of Japanese Studies is engaged in the preparation of teaching materials pertaining to japanese language in addition to the Japanese courses conducted at various levels. The departments of Telugu Studies, Kannada Studies, and Japanese Studies are funded by the Governments of Andhra Pradesh and Karnataka, and several Japanese foundations and individuals respectively.

Publications

The biannual journal issued by the Institute under the name The Journal of the Institute of Asian Studies has played a vital role in pooling together the expertise of various scholars scattered all over the world who are interested in Asian studies. Started in 1983, 24 number of this journal have been released containing large numbers of research papers on various aspects of Asian culture.

The Publications Division if the Institute of asian Studies has been responsible for many books on the cultural heritage of the people of India, especially those of South india. A list of publications can be obtained from the Institute.

Department of Manuscriptology Library

The department of manuscriptology is one of the most important components of this Institute. It is engaged in the collection preservation and publication of rare texts which are

available on fragile palm-leaf and other manuscripts. A tentative survey made by this department pertaining to the palm-leaf manuscripts available in the Tamil language shows that 21% of manuscripts have been published and 79% of them still remain unpublished. These unpublished materials, which are written in a fragile, organic, medium namely palm-leaf, are disintegrating due to human negligence and natural calamities. The department of manuscriptology is engaged in launching projects which are aimed at preserving the cultural treasures of the people of the southern part of India from decay and disintegration. the academic programmes of this department will gradually be expanded to the rare manuscripts available in other parts of Asia. there is a good palm-leaf manuscripts library at the department with large numbers of rare, unpublished work which the Institute is planning to publish one by one with English translation.

This department is also launching a project on the works available in manuscripts dealing with traditional science. One of the main projects of this department is the preparation of a detailed Descriptive Catalogue of Palm-leaf Manuscripts in Tamil in about 25 volumes each consisting of two parts. The first four volumes in eight parts have already been published. The department has also conducted a seminar on the palm-leaf manuscripts available in various Indian languages. The proceedings of this seminar will be published.

The department periodically conducts workshops with a view to imparting training for young scholars in reading and editing the manuscripts.

The Department of Manuscriptology came into being in 1985 thriugh the efforts of Dr (Mrs) Kapila Vatsyayan and Justice V.R. Krishna Iyer.

The objectives of the Department of Manuscriptology are:

1. To host professional seminars and workshops on manuscriptology as well as post-graduate studies and fieldwork in manuscriptology;

2. To preserve palm-leaf manuscripts in which lie embodied ancient knowledge and cultural memories;
3. To collect palm-leaf manuscripts;
4. To establish and maintain a library of palm-leaf manuscripts;
5. To translate palm-leaf manuscripts into English;
6. To store the information derived from palm-leaf manuscripts on a ditigally searchable database (For details: enquire by e- mail)
7. To compile and publish a comprehensive index of palm-leaf manuscripts in 25 volumes;
8. To depute scholars to training programmes on preservation of palm- leaf manuscripts;
9. To record palm-leaf manuscripts on micro-film and other media;
10. To conduct research on traditional sciences;

The IAS Index of Palm-leaf Manuscripts

The Institute is aware of the shortage of reference books on manuscriptology to pursue comparative studies in the field and has taken steps to remedy the situation. Along the lines of the Tamil Department which has begun publishing an Encyclopaedia of Tamil Literature, the Department of Manuscriptology has an ambitious plan of bringing out an Index of palm-leaf manuscripts available on subjects as varied as the history of the Tamil language and literature, Tamil culture, fine arts, logic, astrology, folklore, medicine and magic with a typical Tamil bias. This will be an ideal reference book for scholars engaged in research in their respective fields.

The oldest and perhaps the biggest library of manuscripts, the Government Library of Oriental Manuscripts (Chennai), the U.V. Swaminathaiyar Library, the Saraswathi Mahal Library (Tañjavur) and the Tamil University Library have also brought out indexes to the palm-leaf manuscripts available in the country.

But the information containe d in these catalogues is not exhaustive enough to enable a student of research to make use of it effectively. But the database listing of palm-leaf manuscripts prepared by the Institute of Asian Studies contain all relevant information classified under four categories:

1. In the first category, material description of the manuscript includes the number of leaves it contains, the present condition of the manuscript, the name of the author and the commentator as well as the name of the copyist.
2. The second section can be broadly described as bibliographical description. The date of the publication of the manuscript and the number of editions are given for those that have been printed in book form. In the case of manuscripts which have not been printed, details regarding the use of the information in other printed works, if any, hav e been provided.
3. The third section is devoted to the contents of the manuscript. This may be called subject description. Besides the contents, the genre to which the text belongs, its relevance to the social life of the day, its style and historical associations if any, are detailed. The beginning and ending lines of all the manuscripts are given.
4. The fourth section highlights the uniqueness of the manuscript, its relationship to similar manuscripts, the views of the scholars and also the impact of the manuscript on the writings of others.

Indeed, the Institute of Asian Studies is undertaking a very ambitious project of assembling indices for all the Tamil palm-leaf manuscripts available in the world in 25 volumes, each volume containing two distinct parts. With the co- operation of the Government of India, the Government of Tamil Nadu and the Indira Gandhi Centre for the Developme nt of National Culture, efforts are underway to collect details of palm- leaf manuscripts.

The extent of indexing work to date may be seen in the following table:

Indices of palm-leaf manuscripts

Library	Indexed Manuscripts
Dr U.V. Swaminathaiyar Library	2398
TiruvAvaTutuRai aTINam	1266
Central Research Institute of Siddha Medicine (Chennai)	2149
Madurai Tamil Cankam (Madurai)	389
Tarumapuram aTINam	481
Kalaimakal Kalvi Nilayam (Erode)	133
Theosophical Seminary (Madurai)	159
KumAratEvar maTam (Viruddachalam)	485
Tamil Nadu Siddha Hospital Library (Chennai)	1526
Institute of Asian Studies (Chennai)	1285
Descriptive Catalogues	

To date four descriptive catalogues have been published by the IAS:

Descriptive Catalogue Vol I-II

These two volumes contain the list of palm-leaf manuscripts available in the U.V. Swaminathaiyar Library. The spade work was done by M.K. Raman and later it was exhaustively edited by M. Shanmugam Pillai. The first two volumes containing four parts have been published. These two volumes contain commentary for 2,398 manuscripts.

Descriptive Catalogue Vol III

This lists with commentary the palm-leaf manuscripts available at the TiruvAvaTuturai aTINam Library and is published in two parts. A total of 1266 manuscripts figure in the list. (Part - I. 603 + Part - II. 663 = 1266).

Descriptive Catalogue Vol IV

This Volume covers 815 manuscripts available in the Institute of Asian Studies (part I 438 + part II 377). Most of them have a bearing on the South, to be more precise, most of them belong to Kumari and Nellai Districts.

Descriptive Catalogue Vol V

Vol V Part I contains descriptions of 470 manuscripts available in the Institute of Asian Studies and Vol V part II contains manuscripts available in CRIS, Chennai.

Published Manuscripts in Tamil with English translation

Among the palm-leaf manuscripts preserved in the Institute, fifty are on magic and medicine. More than a hundred are on folklore. Out of this, seventy are ballads. Some of the ballads are being brought out in book form by the Institute. It is proposed to publish many of these manuscripts in book form in the near future.

In the Kerala University Library of Manuscriptology, containing a large number of manuscripts, most of the manuscripts are in the form of ballads collected from the districts of the deep South. Similarly, the manuscripts available in the Institute of Asian Studies also have their origin in the same area. In fact, next to the Kerala University Library of Manuscriptology, the Institute of Asian Studies has the greatest number of manuscripts on folklore. These have largely for their subject matter the glorification of minor deities and their worship. Some fifty manuscripts deal with astrology, yoga, mantra, etc. About twenty manuscripts have bearing on grammar, literature, drama and purANas. There are some manuscripts in the grantha script carrying the titles PushpAñcali, Vakai, KalacApishEkappiracitti, TaNañcaya nikaNTu and yOjANAppiramANam. Their number is about fifty. The descriptive catalogue (Vol IV Part I & II and Vol V Part I) carries the full list.

1. The Wandering Voice

This is the first publication of the Department of Manuscriptology of this Institute. This contains three ballads: CiNNattampi katai, KurukkuLAñci katai, Ucci Nim AkA Liyamman katai. The book carries an English translation and exhaustive notes. The protaganist Chinnathampi, born in a low-caste, falls victim to the greed and the caste disc rimination practised by the upper castes is the theme of the ballad. KurukkuLAñci katai also deals with a social theme. The anxiety of the upper castes to establish the supremacy of the caste system is effectively underlined. The theme of UccinimAkALiyamman borders on fantasy — how Goddess KALi herself tried to annihil ate British power and paved the way for India's independence is poignantly told. The commentary and notes have been prepared by Dr A. Nirmala Devi. Translated by Dr V. Murugan.

2. The Art of Drumming

MattaLam is a percussion instrument very popular in Tamil Nadu. The grammar behind the technique of drumming and the nuances of the sound patterns that can be generated on the instrument have been exhaustively dealt with. Dr Sundaram has based this on a palm-leaf manuscript salvaged by Dr N.Ramachandran Nair from PUta ppANTi.

3. The Dateless Muse - The Story of Venkala RAjan

The Venkala RAjan katai traces the genealogy of the NATAr community. The genesis, growth and the evolution have been described elaborately. Venkala RAjan, the protagonist represents the ethos of the community. His conflict with the upper castes, intrigues and counter intrigues constitute the theme. Incidentally, it throws light on the merits and strong points of various communities besides their weaknesses and shortcomings. Venkala RAjan, who loses his life in the struggle, is verily defied by the community and continues to be held in great respect even today. Translated by Dr V. Murugan.

4. The Unsung Melodies

This has an off-beat theme. Instead of describing the conflict between the upper castes and the lower castes, this concentrates on the intrigues that obtained in the Mar\avar community. How the British cleverly exploited this and captured KaTTapomman constitutes the theme. Translated by Dr V. Murugan

5. Elder Brother's Story ANNanmAr katai Part I & II

ANNanmAr katai tells the story of two brave KauNTar brothers of Coimbatore district with a sociological bias. The story which was popular orally has been compiled and edited with an English translation by Dr Brenda Beck.

6. The Divine Pilgrimage

This is the oldest manuscript in the collection available at the Institute of Asian Studies. This ballad is nearly 300 years old. Lord PerumAL having his abode in Srirankam is going on a pilgrimage to the temple of Padmanabha at Tiruvanantapuram. This journey is used profitably by the author to describe the fauna and the flora of the countries. While Prof. M. Shanmugam Pillai has exhaustively annotated the text, the English translation has been superbly done by Dr J. Parthasarathy.

7. A Tale of Romance - Sakuntalai VilAcam

Published in 1993 the text deals with the well- known story of Shakuntala. The version of Kalidasa has not been followed. The ballad has drawn inspiration from the Shakuntala story figuring in the Mahabharata. Incidentlly, the tale throws light on the social conditions which prevailed in the Kumari district. Edited Dr A. Thasarathan and trans lated by V. Gowri Shankar.

8. Varma CUttiram

Details about the various varmas, the vulnerable points and the drugs to be administered for diseases connected with Varmam are given. This manuscript is published by Dr Shu Hikosaka from the International Institute of Asian Studies, Kyoto.

The English translated has been done by Dr M. Radhika. Dr P. Subramaniam has exhaustively prepared the text ual notes.

9. NiIli yaTcakAnam

YaTcakAnam is a kind of drama resembling the terukkUttu of Tamil Nadu. The Institute proposes to bring out a series of books on YaTcakAnam and this one on PaLayaNUr is the first of the series. The story of NiIli, which has captivated even Buddhists and Jains, has several versions. An English version is published under the title A Tale of Nemesis translated by G.S. Balakrishnan and edited by P. Subrahmaniam.

10. The Valorous Virgins (PeNNaraciyar Katai)

This manuscript, available under the title PurushAtEvi katai at the Institute of Asian Studies, has been exhaustively annotated with textual notes by Dr K. Jayakumar and Mr D. Boominaganathan. The theme has relevance to matriarchal society and the liberation of women. This ballad has great significance in that it dealt with the emancipation of women at a time, some hundred years ago, when such subjects were a taboo. An English version has been released under the title The Valorous Virgins translated by Dr S Mark Joseph.

11. The Epic Eternal (IrAmar katai) Part I & II

Just as Kampa RAmAyaNam drew inspiration from Valmiki's RAmAyaNa and was written to suit the tastes and the temperament of the Tamils, IrAmar katai is a villuppaTTu running to nearly six thousand lines and tailored to suit the needs of the mass. Edited by Dr K. Jayakumar the Institute has brought out an annotated edition of this bow-song, with English translation in two parts done by K.G.Seshadri.

12. The Vows Fulfilled (AmaiyAr ammAnai)

The story line is as follows: The son of NAkamAmuni is born as a tortoise, thanks to his deeds in the previous birth. He marries four women to execute the pledge of his mother. Ultimately he attains salvation. The story abounds in

improbabilities and underlines the importance of divine grace or bliss. This is edited by M. Maruthamuthu and translated by G.S. Balakrishnan.

13. Destiny and Divinity (VarAnkata maharAjan katai)

In VarAnkata maharAjan katai, an attempt is made to propagate the cherished ideals of Jainism. VarAnkatan, the hero is persecuted by his step mother. She even goes to the extent of plotting to murder him. VarAnkatan reveals his nobility by making a sublime sacrifice. The kingly duties, which his father had thrust on him, are transferred to the son of the stepmother after his father's demise. In other words, VarAnkatan crowns his stepbrother as the king. Edited by Mr. M. Parimanan and translated by Dr R. Raja Rathnam.

14. A Tale of Betrayal (CArankataran yaTcakAn\am)

IrajAnarEntaran is the king of IrajamakEntirapuram. CArankataran is his son by the first wife. Due to the intriguing of his wicked stepmother, CArankataran's hands and legs are chopped off. He does not blame anyone and naturally adopts a resigned attitude. This story is very popular in Tamil Nadu both as a ballad and drama. This is the second book which the Institute of Asian Studies proposes to publish under the YaTcakAnam series. Edited by Dr P. Subramaniam and translated by G.S. Balakrishnan.

15. Poetic Petal in the Interior Landscape (UttaNTan kOvai)

This manuscript is edited by R. Jayalakshmi, Research Associate in the Department of Manuscriptology. This belongs to the genre called kOvai and is classified as minor literature. The protagonist is UttaNTan hailing from IrAcakEsari nallUr on the banks of the river PAlAru. This kOvai is divided into 400 sections of akam genre such as love at first sight, hero's suspicion of heroine's beauty. The story of UttaNTan incidentally throws considerable light on the cultural life of TonNTaimaNTalam. Translated by Dr K. Chellappan and Dr P. Paremeswaran.

16. MEril KaruttammaL ammANai

KaruttAL, around whose life the story is woven, is a brave woman with an unusual sense of fortitude. She follows the Christian way of life fervently. Her scholarship in Hinduism helps her and adds an additional dimension to her preaching. Set in the KaliveNpA (a kind of metre), this belongs to the genre called ammAnai , broadly classified as minor literature. Edited by C. Arunachalam and translated by Dr R. Raja Rathnam

17. Where Justice Chimes(TErUrnta cOLan yaTcakANam)

The protagonist is a Cola king setting much store by justice and fair play. Thanks to the blessing of Lord TiyAkEca, the issueless king begets a son who grows up into a young man of parts. Riding a chariot, the prince runs over a calf and kills it. The bereaved mother cow rings the bell of justice quite frantically. the king comes to its rescue. He equates the calf's life with the life of his son and punishes him by running the chariot over him. The kind gods intervene and all ends well. Edited by Dr. P. Subramaniam with English translation by G.S. Balakrishnan. (480 pp.)

Works in progress

Other than the seventeen manuscripts that have been published in book form, the Institute has plans to release another seven books in 1997 on the following titles from YaTcakANam, AmmANai, and Jain literature:

1. TinkaLur MAmalaiyAn noNTinATakam

This work, written by the poet AvinAci, falls under the genre noNTinATakam, one of the kinds of minor literature. It extols the greatness of Lord Murukan, residing in TinkaLUr near Erode. The work that depicts many histrical characters and events is being edited by M. Maruthamuthu.

2. Tirukkalampakam

This text, which belongs to the kalampakam genre of minor

literature, glorifies the greatness of the Jaina god, Aruka tEvar and Jain philosophy. The author of this text is UtIcittEvar. The manuscript is being edited by M. Parimanan.

3. KOlavarittuyilarankan caritam

This manuscript which glorifies the God residing in Cinkapuram, near Ceñci, is being edited by Dr P. Subramaniam and M. Satiyabama.

4. VaikuNTa mmANai

This manuscript which is a sequel to the epic Mahabharatam, depicts the voyage of PANTavas to heaven in AmmAnai form. Editing this manuscript is entrusted with Dr K. Jaya Kumar.

5. TaTciNAmUrtti ValaivAkaTam

Dr P. Subramaniam and Pirasanna have colloborated in editing this medical manuscript available in Anna Hospital.

6. MataNa kAmEcuram

This is another medical manuscript preserved at Anna Hospital. Dr K. Jayakumar and ALakapparAcu are collobarated in editing this manuscript.

Time was when Tamilians recorded their ideas in palm-leaf manuscripts. Thanks to the printing press, this method of preserving knowledge for posterity fell into obsolesence. Still today, surviving palm-leaf manuscripts are store-houses of age-old knowledge and wisdom.

If these palm-leaf manuscripts are to be saved and recorded, it will demand the time of many trained scholars. And yet, there are very few people who know the intricacies of palm-leaf writing and can decipher them. So the urgency to train people to read the manuscripts cannot be minimised. The Institute of Asian Studies has sought the help of the Government of India to run workshops on manuscript reading. Earlier the workshops were held once in two years; now it has become an annual affair.

1. First Workshop on Palm-leaf Manuscript Deciphering

The first workshop was held on 21.3.90 in the presence of the Chairman of the Governing body, Justice V.R. Krishna Iyer. Prof. M. Shanmugam Pillai was the project head. Twenty-five participants were trained over a period of 21 days.

2. Second Workshop on Palm-leaf Manuscript Deciphering

The second workshop was held from 17.2.92 to 9.3.92 and was conducted by Prof. M. Shanmugam Pillai. Most of the people who underwent training were practitioners of the Siddha school of medicine.

3. Third Workshop on Palm-leaf Manuscript Deciphering

This was held from 14.02.94 to 07.03.94. Dr A. Thasarathan was in charge. Mutual exchange of ideas and the work to be done in future were the subjects on the agenda.

4. Fourth Workshop on Palm-leaf Manuscript Deciphering

A fourth workshop was held between 1.3.95 and 21.3.95. Dr P. Subramaniam and Dr K. Jayakumar were in charge of this workshop.

5. Fifth Workshop on Palm-leaf Manuscript Deciphering

The fifth workshop was held between 3.2.97 and 27.2.97 at the new IAS campus. This was conducted by Dr P. Subramaniam and Dr K. Jaya Kumar.

The Usefulness of Workshops - Programme of work

The first few classes of the workshop are devoted to the following topics:

1. What is Manuscriptology?
2. Aims of the workshop
3. Methods employed in the preparation of palm-leaf manuscripts

4. The script
5. Related topics

Next the origin of the Tamil script, its growth, the nature of the script, etc. are exhaustively analysed and discussed. This introduces the student to the art of deciphering the scripts. The letters of the alphabet in the old form, morphology, Tamil numerals, the mixing of Grantha letters with Tamil letters, etc., are then dealt with.

The next stage in the training includes the following topics:

1. variations in texts
2. interpolations
3. examination of the originals
4. word usage
5. methods of publishing palm-leaf manuscripts.

Demonstration lectures with concrete examples follow.

The student is also taught to identify Tamil letters, letters in the Brahmi script, Tamil numerals and Tamil measuring units. The methodology of sorting out the genuine verses from spurious ones on a scientific basis and bringing out an authentic and authoritative translation is taught with reference to subjects as varied as astrology, magic and medicine. The course also includes the interpretation of manuscripts which have a bearing on the teaching of various religious sects such as the Christians, Muslims, Vaishnavites and so on. Enough background information is provided to do this work with skill and competence. Lectures concentrate on the collection of manuscripts from various sources and their preservation. Details about the pioneers in the field of manuscriptology and their interesting experiences go a long way in equipping the student adequately to decipher manuscripts with confidence.

Having acquired this knowledge, trainees visit institutes of manuscriptology and see for themselves a few manuscripts. The most important part of the training programme consists in

assigning to each trainee a manuscript for editing. He or she will be expected to concentrate on every item of publishing including the cover page, front piece, contents, abstract, editorial notes, research notes, interpolations, variations, morphology, etc. The work of each candidate is assessed against an absolute standard of excellence.

The training motivates students to take up the following tasks with great confidence and competence:

* collection of manuscripts
* manuscript preservation
* duties as librarian of an institute of manuscriptology
* duties as a publisher and editor of rare manuscripts

The training also helps one to function effectively as a research scholar by adding to one's range and depth of scholarship. Experts on manuscriptology, eminent epigraphists and specialists in different fields associated with manuscriptology comprise the resource personnel for the workshops.

The Department was started with the idea of examining Tamil palm-leaf manuscripts only, but its range of operation has grown to include other languages as well. This has added to its stature as a regional center of manuscriptology where palm-leaf manuscripts of a diverse nature written in different languages are studied and published authoritative ly. Under the guidance of IAS Director for Research Programmes Dr G. John Samuel, the Department has evolved an ambitious programme to study the scientific truths lying embedded in old palm-leaf manuscripts dealing with diverse subjects like astrology, medicine, architecture, astronomy and geology, among other fields.

UNESCO and the Memory of the World

The United Nations Educational Scientific and Cultural Organisation (UNESCO) has recognised the ongoing contribution of the IAS to the preservation of the world's cultural heritage. In its Memory of the World programme covering all the cultural

relics available in the world, UNESCO has commended the substantial achievements of the Institute of Asian Studies.

The Institute's Director Dr G. John Samuel has been serving on the World Expert Committee of the UNESCO appointed to identify the world's treasure- stores of knowledge since 1993. As India's expert on the World Expert Committee, Dr Samuel has underscored India's unexplored contribution to the world's body of knowledge.

The first meeting of the World Expert Committee was held in Warsaw during 12-14 Sept 1993. At the first meeting, discussion centerd around the memorable relics of the world and various recommendations were made to the General Conference. The memorable relics included rare manuscripts, palm- leaf manuscripts, oral traditions and the knowledge of tho se whose language lacked a script, inventions, unexplored arts and religious practices, beliefs and mores. The need to record and catalogue all the above items was unanimously agreed upon. Subsequent to the Committee meeting in Warsaw, Dr Samuel also participated by invitation in the meeting of the Advisory Committee when it met in Oslo on 1-8 Jun e 1996.

Following the recognition of palm-leaf manuscripts as memorable relics of the world, the Institute of Asian Studies drew up a programme to assess and study the Tamil manuscripts available in the world. It was decided to hold an international seminar to underline the urgency. As a first step, a national seminar on palm-leaf manuscripts was jointly organised by the Institute of Asian Studies and Pondicherry Central University.

Dr A. Pandurangan organised the seminar, which was presided over by Dr Gnanam with keynote address delivered by the Director of the Institute of French Culture, Pondicherry, Dr. Francois Gros. Information regarding palm- leaf manuscripts in Assamese, Oriya, Gujarathi, Sanskrit, Punjabi, Pali, Bengali and Marathi was exchanged. Scholarly papers on palm-leaf manuscripts available in the South Indian languages, namely Kannada, Tamil, Telugu, Tulu and Malayalam were presented.

The Sanskrit manuscripts were discussed separately under two heads: Sanskrit manuscripts available in India those available outside India. The discussion also centred on the denominators of various scripts employed in the palm-leaf manuscripts such as Bengali, Moti and CAratA. There was a presentation concerning palm-leaf manuscripts found in the Raghunath temple in Jammu. Three articles were presented on the collection and preservation of palm-leaf manuscripts. The conference brought to light the places where Tamil manuscripts had been found and highlighted the location of manuscripts in other languages. The proceedings of the seminar were published under the title Palm-leaf and other Manuscripts in Indian Languages in August 1996.

The collecting and preserving of palm-leaf manuscripts

Director of the Institute of Asian Studies Dr G. John Samuel has pioneered the collecting and documenting of palm-leaf manuscripts from diverse sources. Many others like Dr A. Thasarathan, Dr N.Ramachandran, Dr Govindasami, D. Boominaganathan and Pulavar B. Kannaiyan followed his example, collecting many invaluable manuscripts.

Most of the manuscripts that have been collected are from the Southern part of the PaNTyanATu. Thus far, palm-leaf manuscripts have been obtained from the following localities:

4

GOVERNMENT ORIENTAL MANUSCRIPTS LIBRARY, CHENNAI

The Governemnt Oriental Library Madras is located in the Western Wing of the first floor of the Madras University Library. It is unique in respect of its precious holdings and one of the oldest oriental libraries of the country. The Library possess invaluable printed books and manuscripts of many languages in different scripts specially, Tamil, Telugu, Kannada, Marathi, Malayalam and Persian which provided immense knowledge on the history of South India.

The Library was established out of the efforts of Colonel Mackenzie, an Englishman and an engineer by profession. He studied and collected materials on Indian Mathematics and Logarithm as per the instruction of Lord Makinston. He collected a number of documentary sources including manuscripts, coins etc. from 1782 to 1820. After his death, these materials were sold by his wife to the Governor General Marquis Hastings which was went in possession of the East India company and was later sent to Madras and Kolkatta for the Asiatic society.

The collection of the Library increased with the passage of time and the Britishers were the main promoters for it. The Collections of colonel Mackenzie(1754-1821), Dr. Leyden and Mr. C. P. Brown constitute the nucleus of the vast collection of manuscripts preserved in Government Oriental Manuscripts Library, Madras, which consists of manuscripts of works in literature, history, philosophy and science, written in South Indian and Oriental Languages, and of Kaifiyats and inscriptions found in many places belonging to different periods.

The work of preparing catalogues of the manuscripts started in 1873. and since then many volumes have come out. Grants were allocated for the purpose both by the Central as well as State governments. The curator Mr. T. Chandrashekhar played a very active role in bringing out the catalogues of the manuscripts of historical value.

There was a committee of experts called the Editorial Board of the Library which was responsible for identification of the manuscripts of historical value before they were printed in book form. In addition the committee was responsible for selection of books as well as editors. Books were published in series and the two famous series were Madras Government Oriental series and Government Oriental Manuscripts series.The Library has provision of copying of manuscripts through its qualified staff specially appointed for the purpose. It also has a bindery.

The holding of the Library have been divided into collection and these various collections as described below:

Mackenzie's Collection

Colonel Colin Mackenzie who came to India in 1783 as a Cadet of Engineers on the Madras Establishment of the East India Company took a keen interest in the study of ancient mathematics and, of Logarithm in particular, and in Oriental languages. He collected a large number of manuscripts, coins, inscriptions, maps etc., bearing on the liberature, religion, history, manners and customs of the people not only from different parts of India but also from Ceylon and Java.

On his appointment as Surveyor-General of India in 1818, Colonel Mackenzie took his valuable collections with him to Calcutta and went on adding to them till his death in 1821.

This collection was bought from Mrs. Mackenzie for 10,000 pounds by the East India Company in 1821 and divided into three parts. While one part was retained in London, the other parts were sent to Calcutta and Madras.

Leyden's Collection

In 1837, C.P.Brown noticed a collection of manuscripts in Tamil, Telugu and Kannada characters in the India Office Library, London. This invaluable collection belonged to Dr.Leyden, a remarkable linguist and traveller who was in India during 1803-1811. After his death, the East India Company purchased it and lodged at the India House, London. Thanks to the efforts of C.P.Brown, who had joined Indian Civil Service, it was subsequently brought to India.

Brown's Collection

Brown (1798-1184) himself presented to the East India Company his own valuable collections of paper manuscripts of Sanskrit and Telugu works. This collection was brought to India in 1855.

Growth of the Collection

Full fledged library in the true sense was started in 1869. Three collections i.e. the Mackenzie Collection and Brown Collection were transferred to Presidency College, Madras in 1870 and Mr. Pickford who was Professor of Sanskrit in Presidency College, was directed to prepare a Catalogue for them.

He was then called upon to prepare a scheme for publication of important literary and historical manuscripts. In 1876 he was requested to explore for new manuscripts and to purchase or acquire them by transcription.

Accordingly, many manuscripts were acquired from time to time and added to the Library collection.

From such small beginnings, GOML, MADRAS, has grown to its present dimensions and it possesses 71180 manuscripts in the following languages:

Telugu	2150
Sanskrit	48884
Tamil	16398

Kannada	250
Marathi	956
Urdu	184
Arabic	407
Persian	1390
Other Oriental languages	127
Local Records	434
	71180

Consequent on the formation of linguistic States in our country about 7,000 manluscripts in Telugu, Kannada and Malayalam were transferred to Andhra Pradesh, Karnataka and Kerala respectively. Apart from this 22,887 printed books are available for reference in the Library.

Functions

The main functions of GOML are as follows:

1. Acquisition and preservation of manuscripts.
2. Classification and Cataloguing of manuscripts.
3. Publication of rare manuscripts and Library Catalogues.
4. Purchase of books and periodicalsl for reference, and
5. Supply of information of manuscripts to the scholars.

Preservation

The rare and valuable palm-leaf manuscripts are carefully preserved by adopting manual and chemical methods. The injured and damaged paper manuscripts are preserved by being mended with Chiffon cloth.

Publications

GOML has brought out so far 350 publications including Descriptive and Triennial Catalogues of its manuscripts in various languages. The publication have been broughtl under two series. GOVERNMENT ORIENTAL MANUSCRIPTS SERIES and

GOVERNMENT ORIENTAL SERIES, those in the latter being edited by the Curator and the staffr of the Library.

Bulletin

Multilingual Bulletin published annually by GOML contains in-print, rare and unpublished manuscripts in various languages. Twenty one volumes have been published so far.

Participation in Exhibition

The rare and valuable manuscripts of GOML were displayed in the manuscript exhibitions on the following occasions:

1. 1964 - The Twenty Sixth International Congress of Orientalists in New Delhi.
2. 1964 - The Third All India Agama Silpa Bharata Forklore Conference in Kancheepuram.
3. 1965 - The World Telugu Conference in Hyderabad
4. 1968 - The Second World Tamil Conference in Madras.
5. 1968 - The Lord Mahaveera's 25th Parinirvana Centenary Celebrations in Madras
6. 1980 - The Silver Jubilee Celebrations of the Sanskrit Department Vevekananda College in Madras
7. 1980 - The Chitirai Festival in Madurai
8. 1981 - The Fifth World Tamil Conference in Madurai
9. 1982 - Seminar on Sanskrit Literature at Vivekananda College in Madras

GOML is a government institution headed by the Curator under the control ofl the Director of Archaeology, Government of Tamilnadu.

Service

Manuscripts and books are issued to visitors for study or consultation on request. Permission is accorded to research scholars for studying, copying and comparing the manuscripts.

5

SARASWATI MAHAL LIBRARY, TANJORE

Tanjore or Thanjavur as it was earlier called, was the capital of the chola empire from the 10th century to the 14th century A.D. later is become part of the Vijaynagar kingdom, then passed into the hands of the Marathas and later still went to the British. For ages it has been the chief political, literary and religious centre of the South. The celebrated temple Brihadeshra built by the Chola King during the 11th century is its major attraction. The Saraswati Mahal Library, dating back from the time of the Marathas, contains a rare collectins of books and manuscripts on paper and plam leaves.

The Library has been named after Maharaja Serfoji's. It is located at the palace of the Maharaja. The Library contains paper manuscripts on different subjects such as science, medicine, engineering, astronomy, painting, dancing, etc. in various languages such as Sanskrit, Tamil, Telugu, Marathi and some European languages. Around 8,000 of these are on palm leaves. This is the result of the efforts of the Nayak and Maratha rulers for over 300 years. This palace library was originally developed by the Nayak rulers. The Maratha rulers especially Raja Serfoji made a major contribution, organising a massive collection of good books.

The question of treating the Library as an institution of national importance has been under consideration. It was suggested to the Government of Tamil Nadu that the management of the Library should be entrusted to a body to be set up under an Act of Parliament on the pattern of the Board of the Khuda Bakhsh

Oriental Public Library, Patna. The reply from the present Government of Tamil Nadu for entrusting the management of the said library to a high powered Board is awaited. The Government of India have set up a small committee to assess the financial requirements of the Library and also make recommendations for its future development. The Report of Committee was accepted by the Government of India. The main recommendation of the Committee deals with purchase of equipment for lamination famigation, microfilming, reprography and for air conditioning of selected portions for preservation of manuscripts. A recurring annual expenditure of Rs. 3 lakhs (approximately) is to be borne by the Government of India for the maintenance of the Library in addition to the grant of Rs. 57,500 which the Government of Tamil Nadu have agreed to pay to this Library.

In the old days palm-leaf manuscripts were preserved in almost every house. They contained the texts of the epics, the Puranas, Sthala Puranas, and so on. When the palm-leaves were in danger of being damaged, their contents would be copied with a stylus on new leaves. The damaged leaves would be consigned to the Kaveri or some other sacred river, or to some pond on the occasion of Patinettam Per.

The Library has been described by Dr. Burnell " to be perhaps the largest and the most important in the World" and which Dr. Buhler says " contains a great many useful and a number of many rare or nearly unique books many of which are quite unknown or procurable only with great trouble and expense". It was a private property earlier under the possession of Rajas of Tanjore.

The Beginning of the Library

The earliest beginning of the Library must have been about the end of the 16th century when Tanjore was under the rule of Telugu nayakas who collected Sanskrit manuscripts written in Telugu characters. In the eighteenth century the Marathas

conquered the country and since then the Library has been increasing. By far the greater portion of the collection was made by Serfoji during a visit to Benaras during 1820 to 1830. Sivaji, his successor added a few. There has practically been no addition of any value till recent times. A good number of Sanskrit manuscripts including rare and valuable manuscripts representing the collection of generations of a family of scholars known as "Jumbunatha Bhatt, Landagai collection" was added to the Library in 1921.

The attention of the Government of India and through it the Government of Madras was directed in 1868 to the importance of the examination, purchase or transcription of manuscripts in Sanskrit language available in Indian libraries and the framing of printed lists or catalogue of the same. In December of the same year, the Government of Madras asked Mr. Pickford, Professor of Sanskrit to carry out the instructions of the government of India. He commenced to catalogue the manuscripts at Tanjore; but he felt seriously ill and had to return to Europe in March 1870 and never came back to India. It is not known how much he had done as his unfinished catalogues could not be found.

Thereupon Dr. Burnell, District and Session Judge, was appointed to catalogue Sanskrit manuscripts at Tanjore. This learned scholar devoted a great deal of research and labour to the task and his catalogue which he styled " a classified index to the Sanskrit manuscripts in the Palace at Tanjore" was published in three parts between 1878 and 1880 in London. This is now chief key to the Sanskrit collection in this Library. But unfortunately great many manuscripts, above 4000, seem to have been omitted and his catalogue cannot be said to be complete.

It is became a public library in the full sense of that term, because the Government of Madras through the treasurer of the Charitable endowments being responsible for its administration. The collection belonged to the reigning princes of Tanjore-the Maratha Maharajas. When the least of them died leaving no direct male heir and after the death of the last surviving Rani, this

collection together with the other properties formed the subject of litigation in civil courts. The collection attracted the attention of some wealthy patron of learning from other countries. And it would appear that arrangements were very nearly ready to sell the whole collection outright at an assessed value, when public attention was focused on certain remarks of Dr. Burnell to the effect that "it would not be possible to form a collection like that at Tanjore at a less cost than L 50,000. The parties concerned had perforce to wake up and the deal was not immediately concluded. The public of Tanjore also began to take interest in the affairs adequately. Then the Government of Madras took possession of the collection under the Charitable Endowments Act in 1918.

In respect of the magnitude and the range of subjects dealt with, not to speak the diversity of languages employed, the Tanjore Library is perhaps second to none among oriental libraries of the country.

As regard the origin of collection, Dr. Hultzsch has the following interesting information in "No. 3 report on Sanskrit manuscripts in Southern India " edited by him in 1905 at Madras:

"The manuscripts described in the report belong to Jumbunathan Bhatta, a Maratha brahmana at Tanjore, who is the elder son of a certain Mannabhatta. He is a no mean Sanskrit scholar and knows the whole Rig Veda by heart. As he is continually teaching the text of this sacred book to students, even his blind daughter has learnt recite portion of it. The existence of this Library was brought to my notice by Mr. T. S. Kuppuswami Sastri, of the Educational Department, who is favorable known to Sanskritists by his paper on Rama Bhadra Dikshita. During my absence furlough in Europe, my first assistant, Mr. V. Venkayya, M A was deputed to Tanjore in order to catalogue Jambunathas collection. He spent three months at this work, in which he received the valuable help of Mr. Kuppuswamy Sastri. Both the lists and the extracts testify to the thoroughness at care with which he has accomplished his task."

In 1922 the Library received other valuable collection of rare interest, known as the "Kagalkar" and the 'Patanga Avadhuta" collections. The former is about 159 and the later, about hundred years old. The collection made by the Kagalkar family of learned Sanskrit scholars specially worst in Sanskrit grammar contains the auto graph copies made some of them of the works composed by themselves and others. Its prominent feature is the collection of works on Sanskrit grammar. The collection made by Patangavadhuta whose descendents settled at Tiruvadamarudur in Tanjore district contains a large number of works on Vedanta and bhakti. Both these collections comprise several manuscripts whose do not exist in this Library. There has been a marked improvement in the working of the Library ever since it became a public trust. Many influential persons came forward and took interest in its development. The manuscripts are either on palm leave or on paper. They are of very different value and have come from many sources. A large collection of them are recent Nagari copies of manuscripts in South Indian characters and are at least are a century old.

These manuscripts are in more than eleven distinct alphabets being from all parts of India. On the whole, one may easily say that the total number of manuscripts in this library is likely to accede.

A large number of original records belonging to the last reigning house of Tanjore which will be of very great importance for reconstructing the political and social history of Maratha rule in Southern India has recently been transferred to the care of this Library from the civil court by the order of the judge.

Nature of Collection

India has a long tradition of creating and preservation of knowledge for the posterity. The earlier generations of the Indians went on inscribing on palm - leaves with their stylus until their hands ached. They copied old texts to be preserved for posterity. This tradition lasted until perhaps the time of our fathers. People

of our generation have thrown these precious manuscripts into the river without making copies of them. So much so it is doubtful whether the texts of many Puranas will ever be available to us. Not only Puranas, but also a number of sastras. However, some scholars have taken great pains to go from place to place to collect manuscripts and preserve them in libraries. The Sarasvati Mahal Library in Tanjavur, the Oriental Manuscripts Library and the Adyar Library, Madras, have good collections of manuscripts. The Theosophical Society Library, Adyar, has done commendable work in this respect. Sarabhoji and other rulers of Tanjavur took great trouble to collect manuscripts for the Sarasvati Mahal.

A large number of the manuscripts in the Library are on palm leaves. The palm-leaf is called edu in Tamil. It has two sides with a rib in between - either of the two sides after the removal of the rib is called an edu. The plantain leaf also has a rib. When it is split across the rib, each part is an edu. For long the palm-leaf was our paper, nature's paper which was not easily damaged. The letters had to be inscribed on it with a stylus.

The palm-leaves containing the text of Jnanasambandhar's Tevaram compositions went upstream against the current of the river Vaigai and were laid ashore. The spot where the manuscript lodged itself is called "Tiruvedakam" ("Tiru +edu + akam"). Here the deity lord Siva is called "Patrika Paramesvara". Nowadays the word "paper" is understood as a newspaper, magazine, periodical, etc. "Patrika" means a magazine today. The lord associated with the spot where the palm-leaves, nature's paper, were laid ashore is "Patrika Paramesvara", which could be taken to mean "the Lord the journalist". "Patra" and "Patrika" mean the same, a leaf. In the past letters were written on palm-leaves. That is why a letter also came to be called "patra".

There is an interesting story about the Sarasvati Mahal. In olden days the worst injury an invader thought he could inflict on a country was to burn down it's libraries. When the treasury is to the economy of the nation the library is to its culture; indeed

the library represents its cultural treasury. Since there was no printing press then, there would not be many [palm-leaf] copies available of works, and of some works there would be only a single copy. To destroy the library of the nation, containing rare works, would be a greater outrage than looting its treasury or dishonouring its women. We must be proud of the fact that our sastras on policy strictly forbid the destruction of an enemy country's treasures of knowledge and it's places of worship, nor do they permit the dishonouring of its women.

When Jainas like Amarasimha lost to Hindu religious teachers in arguement, they themselves wanted to burn their books. But great men like the Acarya stopped them from doing so. Holding the hands of their opponents they requested them not to destroy their books. Their attitude was that no work must be destroyed whatever the philosophy or religious system it upholds.

Conquerers belonging to other countries took special delight in setting fire to the libraries of the conquered land if it was known to be culturally advanced. They perpetrated such outrages without reflecting for a moment on the fact that knowledge is common to all, even such knowledge as possessed by an enemy. They could cause anguish to the people intellectually superior to them by destroying their books.

The Englishmen, Frenchmen and others had a thirst for knowledge and research and were anxious to learn even from foreign sources. The Germans came to our country and searched for palm-leaf manuscripts to take home with whom. We must be grateful to some of these foreigners through whose efforts a number of our sastras were rediscovered. There was, for example, Mackenzie who was surveyor-general of India. He went from place to place to collect palm-leaf manuscripts. There was at that time no special department to deal with them but Mackenzie had them read by experts and took steps to have them preserved. Mackenzie's men even came to our Matha at Kumbakonam to gather information.

It is believed that Westerners took with them some of our science manuscripts from the Sarasvati Mahal especially those pertaining to the art of warfare. It is further claimed that Hitler made some type of weapons and aircraft on the basis of knowledge contained in these texts.

There are palm-leaf manuscripts still with us like Bhojaraja's Samarangana Sutra. From these we learn that we had long ago not only "astras" to be employed with mantras but also "sastras" that were product of science. Digests like Varahamihira's Brhatsamhita bring together the various disciplines of our land.

Some of our ancient palm-leaf manuscripts contain texts not only of our religious systems but also of various arts and sciences. But we have lost many of our Sthala Puranas. We must do our best to preserve what remains and, at the same time, continue the search for more manuscripts.

The Puranas give us instruction, in the form of engrossing stories, on the truth of the Paramatman proclaimed by the Vedas, the dharmas, and the moral and ethical codes of conduct that they lay down. The teaching they impart touches our very hearts. The lessons of the Puranas, the stories of noble men and women contained in them, have shaped our lives. The Puranas have indeed served as a source of our inspiration for our people from time immemorial. We must no longer be apathetic to them and must make a determined effort to preserve them as a treasure. Let us make a comparative study of puranic literature and take an integrated view. This will be to our own benefit as well as to that of all mankind.

Preparation of Catalogues

The Library holds a large number of books and manuscripts in almost all Indian and European languages and almost on all branches of human knowledge. Special mention here may made to the books and manuscripts in Telugu, Tamil, Mararthi and English on account of their number and importance. Dr. Burnell

issued what he modestly styled " A classified index to the Sanskrit manuscripts in the Palace at Tanjore", between 1878 and 1880. Between 1880 and 1918 for very nearly 40 years, the Library has been the victim of many an outrage. Those who were in possession gave out of loan many rare manuscripts which did not return to the Library. A Committee appointed by the Government of Madras took charge of the Library early in 1919. Since then they have been busy pushing forward the work of revising and publishing fresh catalogue of all the works available in the Library. According to the latest scientific methods. Each work is described in detail in a card index form which contains all the necessary particulars.In 1920 a catalogue of printed book in French, Latin, Italian and Greek was published. In 1926 three volumes of a catalogue of Tamil manuscripts in the Library were published. From the year 1924 a catalogue of Mararhi manuscripts and books of the Library was prepared: the first volume was published at that time. the catalogues are available on sale.Administrative Committee of the Library approached the Government of Madras, year after year with the request for a special grant to prepare and publish the descriptive catalogue of Sanskrit manuscripts in the Library. In 1927, the government allotted the necessary funds for a three year programme for carrying out the work of preparing and printing of the catalogue.

Present Collection

The Library has been enriched with several very fine collections of manuscripts every one of them rare, valuable and very interesting manuscripts. The Kagalkal collection, Jambunatha Bhatt Landagaya collection and the Patanga Avadhuta collection on these three alone numbers 2181 manuscripts. Besides these, the Tyagaraj Swamy collection which alone contain more than thousand manuscripts than the minor collections/the Subramanya Sastri collection, Subramaniya Rao collection, Ramchandra Ganapat collection, Neelakantha Sasri collectionTawker Collection, Mehta Ccollection all are of great and paramount importance.Now, the Thanjavur Maharaja Serfoji

Saraswati Mahal Library, Thanjavur has a rich collection of manuscripts numbering 40,000 in Sanskrit, Marathi, Telugu, Tamil and other languages. Besides manuscripts, it has a collection of over 23,000 books in the Indian and European languages covering various disciplines. There is a large number of illustrated manuscripts in Saraswati Mahal Library, Tanjavur, Tamil Nadu. Long before the illustrated story telling began in the modern era, multi-colour paintings, drawings and sketches have embellished manuscripts. While such illustrated manuscripts, several centuries old, are available throughout India, the Archives of IGNCA has a collection of about 800 slides from select illustrated manuscripts in the Saraswati Mahal Libra The Library also hold a large number of books and manuscripts in almost all Indian and European languages and almost on all branches of human knowledge. Special mention here may made to the books and manuscripts in Telugu, Tamil, Mararthi and English on account of their number and importance.Dr, Burnell issued what he modestly styled " A classified index to the Sanskrit manuscripts in the Palace at Tanjore", between 1878 and 1880. Between 1880 and 1918 for very nearly 40 years, the Library has been the victim of many an outrage. Those who were in possession gave out of loan many rare manuscripts which did not return to the Library. A Committee appointed by the Government of Madras took charge of the Library early in 1919. Since then they have been busy pushing forward the work of revising and publishing fresh catalogue of all the works available in the Library. According to the latest scientific methods. Each work is described in detail in a card index form which contains all the necessary particulars.In 1920 a catalogue of printed book in French, Latin, Italian and Greek was published. In 1926 three volumes of a catalogue of Tamil manuscripts in the Library were published. From the year 1924 a catalogue of Mararhi manuscripts and books of the Library was prepared: the first volume was published at that time. the catalogues are available on sale.Administrative Committee of the Library approached the

Government of Madras, year after year with the request for a special grant to prepare and publish the descriptive catalogue of Sanskrit manuscripts in the Library. In 1927, the government allotted the necessary funds for a three year programme for carrying out the work of preparing and printing of the catalogue.ry. The slides are from four manuscripts selected from the list. They are: 1 Nayaka nayaki bhava 2. Citra Ramyana 3. Prabodha Chandrodaya 4.Bhavartha RamayanaThese illustrations are not a mere visual treat. They tell their own story about the date of the manuscripts, the social customs, costumes, jewellery, adornments, the hairstyles, the colour techniques and painting styles. It is with a view to make there accessible to researchers that IGNCA had undertaken a project of slide documentation of the illustrations of the manuscripts, though the entire manuscript collection has been microfilmed. These slides have been arranged in the order of series. For instance, the horse series, bird series, nayaka nayaki bhava, Hindu mythology, palanquins, Rg Veda manuscripts etc. This way the illustrations can be approached in two ways. Reader who knows the title of the manuscript can reach them, or researcher, for a comparative study can pursue a series, a theme, in various manuscripts. The maximum number of slides are in the Hindu mythology series followed by horses. Some precious manuscripts of Maratha origin are in this library. There are 26 slides of illustrations from these. The slides collection does not cover the entire illustrated manuscripts collection. Only some select manuscripts were allowed to be photographed for the purpose. While anyone can see the slides for interest and reference in IGNCA, the permission to publish them rests with the Saraswati Mahal Library.

6
KHUDA BAKHSH ORIENTAL PUBLIC LIBRARY, PATNA

Bakhsh Oriental Public Library was founded by Maulvi Khuda Bakhsh Khan who donated his entire personal collection to the nation by a deed of trust. It was opened for public in October, 1891 by his son with 4,000 manuscripts, of which he inherited 1,400 from his father Maulvi Mohammed Bakhsh Acknowledging its rich and rare collection the Govt. of India declared the Library as an Institution of National Importance by an act of Parliament in 1969. The Library is now fully funded by the Dept. of Culture (Ministry of Tourism and Culture, Govt. of India). Now,, this autonomous institution is governed by a Board with the Governor of Bihar as its ex-officio Chairman and the responsibility of day-to-day management of Library affairs is being carried by Director, Khuda Bakhsh Library.

Maulvi Mohammad Bakhsh, hailed from Chapra, a district of Bihar. He was a man of letters and law and had a great passion for books. He collected about 1,400 manuscripts including some rare printed books. When he was on his death-bed in 1876 he entrusted the whole lot to his son and wished him to open a library for the public whenever he should find himself in a position to do so. Khuda Bakhsh, thus, inherited from his father love for books and dedication to public service. He made it a mission of life to establish a public library so as to fulfil his father's dream. He made all possible efforts to acquire rare books and manuscripts. He also borrowed services of a book-hunter to collect manuscripts from the learning centres in the Arab world. He devoted himself to this noble cause.

With the acquisition of books he laid foundation of a two-storied building for the library. It was ready in 1888 at the cost of Rs. 80,000 and the books were shifted to this newly-constructed beautiful building. To fulfil the long-cherished desire of his father, Khuda Bakhsh opened it for the people of Patna rare manuscripts in Arabic, Persian and Turkish, apart from the printed books in Arabic, Persian and English.

The library was donated to the public and the Govt. of Bengal was made its trustee. It was modestly named as Oriental Public Library according to the Trust Deed. The people, however, prefixed his name in view of his great service to the public. Since then it is officially known as Khuda Bakhsh Oriental Public Library. But popularly it is called Khuda Bakhsh Library.

Khuda Bakhsh was born in Chapra on 2nd August 1842, Khuda Bakhsh and was brought up under the guidance of his father who dedicated his life for the betterment of humanity. Educated at Patna and Calcutta he started his professional career as Peshkar. In 1880 he was appointed the Government Pleader of Patna and in 1881 the title of Khan Bahadur was conferred upon him for his social service. He was elevated to the post of Chief Justice of Nizam's Court Hyderabad for a period of three years in 1895. He was also honored with another title of CIE in 1903. In spite of having all these titles and honours he was a very simple man with determination and vision. The library was his life-long achievement for which he was committed and devoted. He spent whatever he earned on its growth and as a result he was penniless. He had to borrow money for his medical treatment.

The Government of Bengal made him a generous grant of Rs. 8,000 to liquidate his debts. He died on 3rd August 1908 at the age of 66, and was buried in the premises of the Library.

The 26th Dec'1969 was a turning point in the annals of the Library when it was raised to the status of an Institution of National Importance by an Act of Parliament. Being an autonomous body it has been working since then under the control

of the Govt. of India, Department of Culture, Ministry of Tourism and Culture. The raised status played an important role in accelerating the pace of overall development of the library over the years.

Reference service is extended through fax, phone and now through the e-mail also. Normally the correspondence is resorted for long-range reference service. Those, who prefer to come to the Library, are served with full attention and care. Books are also lent out to the members only against their library cards. Curzon Reading Room named after Lord Curzon is open for all. A large number of newspapers and magazines in English, Urdu and Hindi are made available there. Recently reference books and books for competitive exams have also been added to this Reading Room.

Earlier, this reading room was available for only six and a half-hours a day. But now, for the last one year, it remains open for 12 hours a day, i.e., from 8 am to 8 pm to overcome to some extent the paucity of reading space. At an average, more than 9,500 readers visit CRR every month. Under its modernisation programme, the Library has already established its own web-site for the benefit of its readers throughout the world.

Entire collection of catalogues has been fully scanned and published with the help of NIC, Bihar State Unit both on its web-site as well as on CD-ROMs which is available to the local visitors for fast and efficient search of articles of their interest.

Publications

A very special feature of Khuda Bakhsh Library is its publications which have created history in the academic world. Since 1977 it has been issuing regularly a multi-lingual research quarterly Khuda Bakhsh Library Journal. The main aim of bringing out this Journal is to advance research in Oriental and Islamic studies and also to promote research in Literature. Hence it includes scholarly articles, reprints of articles from old research periodicals and prints original articles on the subjects in which the library specializes.

Simultaneously, the Library also undertook a project of publishing research treatises, its manuscripts after getting them edited by scholars, facsimile edition of manuscripts, indices of Urdu periodicals, catalogue of the manuscripts, books bridging the communal gap and also books on Indian culture, history, literature and Islam.

It has brought out so far about 400 titles in the following languages

* Arabic
* Hindi
* English
* Persian
* Urdu

About thirty collections of manuscripts and books have so far been acquired as donation from the owners in addition to those purchased by the Library. The Printed collection has, on the other hand, its own value covering a wide spectrum of subjects such as memoirs, biographies, Tibb, Hinduism and other oriental topics in English, Arabic, Persian, Urdu and Hindi, etc. One significant part of this collection is the Periodical Section which contains around 35,000 bound volumes of old and new periodicals. It is very much used by the scholars and even you can go through it by paying a visit to the Library.

Khuda Bakhsh Library is not merely a library, it is in fact a nucleus of multi-dimensional activities. It caters to the needs of intellectuals and scholars, promotes research, advocates communal harmony and also serves public. During the last fifty years it has organised about 200 extension lectures, talks, group discussions and debates. Eminent personalities have delivered lectures on a variety of subjects.

International seminars have been organised on manuscript literature on Tibb (Unani Medicine), Tasawwuf (Islamic Mysticism), Quranic sciences, Medieval Indian history followed by the seminars on Urdu Manuscripts and on Indo-Uzbek

relations. Free India and Dr. Zakir Husain were the topics for national seminars. Besides, symposia on Reservation for Muslims and Indian Woman have also been arranged in the library.

Several talks have been organized on health care and hygiene specially for public awareness. The library also arranges National and International Mush'ara's (poetry recitation), Kavi Sammelans and Qawwalis besides film shows representing Indian culture and also documentaries.

Khuda Bakhsh struggled throughout his life for communal harmony. The library thus represents this quality of the Founder through its collection and holds group discussions on the issue. The Library has been recognized as a Research Centre by seven Universities, namely –

* Shantiniketan University, Calcutta
* Hamdard University, New Delhi
* Kashmir University, Srinagar
* Gulbarga University, Gulbarga, Karnataka
* Magadh University, Gaya
* B. R Ambedkar University, Muzaffarpur
* Jamia Millia Islamia, New Delhi

Promotion of Research Work

The Library encourages scholars and provides them all research facilities including free accommodation. It awards 10 research fellowships - 3 Senior and 7 Junior - for a period of 2 years and helps them do Ph.D./D.Litt. It also assigns different projects to them, for example, editing of manuscripts, compilation of descriptive catalogue of manuscripts, indexes of Urdu periodicals, subject bibliographies, etc. Besides, it also offers lump sum amount to retired professors to work on our manuscripts.

The Library has started a 1 year PG Course in Oriental Librarianship and Manuscriptology to help produce well trained staff to manage any oriental library. Three batches comprising

of people selected mostly from in-house staff has been successfully concluded and work is going on to improve the scope of this course even further. The Library facilitates exchange of scholars with other countries and takes steps for sharing its resources with other libraries either in India or outside to enrich its collection.

The Library arranges exhibitions of its collection from time to time. It keeps on regular display new arrivals. Apart from the exhibition of books, it has also displayed its rare calligraphic masterpieces, gorgeous paintings and manuscripts on Quraniyat (Quranic sciences) and, Islamic sciences at different occasions in the library. Books on Indic religions have also been kept on display in National Museum, New Delhi

Library Infrastructure

Khuda Bakhsh Library was housed initially in the two-storeyed building that was constructed by its founder in 1888. During the earthquake of 1934, the upper storey toppled down making things very difficult for both the Library and its visitors. In 1938, the State Govt. of Bihar got erected a building on the library campus itself and subsequently, all the books were shifted over to this new building. To resolve the problem of space due to ever expanding collection of Library, another floor was added to the building by the Govt. of India in 1969. Hardly 13 years later, a 3-tier annexe was built-up at the rear of the Library. It was inaugurated on 12th February, 1983 by Shri Giani Zail Singh, the then President of India.

A building in Makhaniya Kuan outside the library campus was purchased to provide accommodation to scholars who come to the library for their research work.

Air-conditioning of manuscript area has been taken up on utmost priority. Envisaging water scarcity, tube-well has already been sunk to provide an alternate reliable source of water supply. Microfilming Section is equipped with Hirakawa Camera, Automatic Processor and Microfilm Reader Printer. Photostat

machine was replaced by Xerox machine in 1985 to improve the reprographic services.

Khuda Bakhsh aspired to have a printing press to make copies of the rare material available to the scholars at distant places. He himself could not do so due to lack of resources. To satisfy the Founder's desire, a M.O.I. mini-offset printer was acquired to print Library Journals and small books. To cope with the increasing amount of printing work and also for better quality of printed work, a bigger offset printing machine was bought last year. It is also used to reproduce out of print material for research purpose.

The library has again reached its saturation point and as a result further development and growth is being hampered. Some personal collections have been offered but could not be accepted due to paucity of space. A plan of six-storied building plan costing Rs. 5.74 Crores has been submitted to the Dept. of Culture (Govt. of India) for approval. The government is expected to take an urgent action to remove all hindrances coming in the way of its development.

Modernization was introduced in the Library as early as 1950's with the provision of Reprographic Services. Other equipments such as electronic typewriter, calculating machines and fumigation chambers were added to the library gradually.

A small Conservation Lab is attached to the rare collection for fumigation, deacidification, lamination and binding. This is to be modernized with latest equipments. Fumigation chamber with latest techniques and impregnator (Lamination machines are on the list of purchase). Cutting and tooling machines are also to be acquired for quality binding.

To computerize the entire library stock and provide online service, a major project was prepared in consultation with National Informatics Centre (NIC), Delhi and Patna and submitted to the Department of Culture for approval. With the generous grant from DOC, a computer centre was set up in 1999.

This was one of the major events coming on heels of the dawn of the new century. This computer centre is equipped with the following items –

* SCO Unix Server
* Modern Pentium based systems (13 Nos.)
* Colour DeskJet Printers
* Scanners
* Digital Camera
* Laser Printer
* LCD Data Projector

All the computer systems and peripherals have been interconnected through LAN for better sharing of resources. E-Mail facility via internet has also become available with the Library. Digitization of Descriptive Catalogue of Manuscripts has already been completed and it has been published over the Internet for global dissemination.

National Informatics Centre is a leading Govt. of India setup in the field of Information Technology. For the last several years, it has played a crucial role in changing the work culture within the govt. organization by the induction of IT-Tools at almost each level of govt. administration.

Publication of catalogues of manuscripts with the Library onto CDs has largely been possible through expert help provided free of cost by NIC Bihar State Unit and they have promised to make available any kind of technical assistance as and when required by the Library in its computerization programme.

Collections of the Library

Presently, the Library holds about 2,25,000 books in Urdu, Persian, Arabic and Hindi languages. It subscribes to 527 Journals. There are about 12,000 volumes of serials which has great value in research. As far as the collection of manuscripts is concerned, the Library holds about 22,000 invaluable manuscripts. Now one of the richest collections of Arabic and

Persian manuscripts and Mughal and Central Asian paintings-presently possessing the Khuda Bakhsh Library is fast becoming a centre foı preserving and dissemination of knowledge in its special fields of Arabic and Persian learning and Islamic and Medieval Indian Studies.

The Library, with its relentless efforts of acquisition, preservation and dissemination, has emerged as one of the richest collections of Persian and Arabic manuscripts, and of rare printed books and invaluable paintings of Mughals, Rajputs, Turkish and Iranian schools. With over a hundred years of service to the world of scholarship and keeping pace with modern concept of librarianship, the Khuda Bakhsh has also brought into the gamut of its services such activities as may play significant role both on the national and the international planes-using knowledge for the betterment of humanity at large, rising above the traditional concept of the Library, the Khuda Bakhsh has become a centre of academics for acquisition of knowledge and dissemination of ideas and ideals. Scholarly workshops, symposia, talks, lectures and, of course, its yearly international seminars have been successfully creating research-based awareness of knowledge both on national and international levels.

Audio and Video Collection

The Library has also build up a comprehensive collection of audio and video cassettes of distinguished writers and poets, and eminence of Ganga-Jamni composite culture. Mass Communication Research Centre, Jamia Millia Islamia, New Delhi has extended cooperation in serving this national cause by making video films of such eminent persons and events that have not been covered directly by the Khuda Bakhsh. Maintaining its pace to record the living eminent poets and writers the sub-continent, the Library had added a large number of cassettes both audio and video to its collection,

With a century long span of services to scholarship to the nation and the humanity at larger, the Khuda Bakhsh remains

the centre of attraction for seekers of knowledge from round the globe with something worthy to offer to every one from its priceless collection of manuscripts, original paintings and rare printed books in oriental as well as in English, French and German languages.

Acquisition of significant material relevant to the Library's specialized fields is a regular feature of the Library. With efforts spread over two decades of persuasion and pleading the following collections have so far been acquired since its take over by the Union Government:

1. Khujwa Collection (Sewan)
2. Idara Tehqiqat-iUrdu Collection (Patna)
3. Dr. Shamim Collection (Arrah)
4. Prof Akhtar Oranvi Collection (patna)
5. All India Radio Collection (Patna)
6. Kako Collection (Gaya)
7. Koniber Collection (Navada)
8. Prof. Kalimuddin Collection (Patna)
9. Sor Fakhruddin Collection (Patna)
10. Khanqah Sulaimania Collection (Patna)
11. Dr. A. R. Kidwai Collection (Patna)
12. Mr. Yunus Salim Collection
13. S. A. Slam Collection (Patna)
14. Ahid Sajjad Jafri Collection (Bihar Sharif)
15. Sabzposh Collection (Gorakhpur)
16. Madrasa Azizia Collection (Bihar Sharif)
17. Sughra Estate Collection (Bihar Sharif)
18. Khanqah Qadiriya Collection (Islampur)
19. Khalid bib Saeed Collection (Bihar Sharif)
20. Zainul Abidin Collection. Chapra
21. Sasaram Collection

22. Dr. Zaki ul Haque Collection (Patna)
23. Ahmad Husain Collection (Sahasram)
24. Iran Coleection (Iranian Students at Patna)
25. Kalimur Rehman Collection (Begu Sarai)
26. Hakim Syed Yusuf Collection (Phulwar Sharif)
27. Qutubuddin Collection (Sahsram)
28. Muzaffar Gilani Collection (Patna)
29. Zainuddin Collection (Saharsa)

There are some more collections. These significant collection are besides the acqusition of books and manuscripts through regular purchase. These includes:

Akhtar Ansari Collection (Aligarh)

Saeed Akbarabadi Collection (Aligarh)

Mukhtaruddin Ahmad Collection (Aligarh)

Meher Iolahi Collection (Aligarh)

Kalam Haidri Collection (Gaya)

The Library specializes in Islamic Studies, Tibb (Unani Medicine), Tazkira (Biography), Tasawwuf (Islamic Mysticism), Comparative religions, Medieval History, South East Asian History, West Asian History, Central Asian History, Medieval Science, Literature on Freedom Movement and National Integration as also Urdu, Persian and Arabic Literatures.

It contains valuable manuscripts in Arabic, Persian, Urdu, Turkish, Hindi and Sanskrit and Palm-Leaves. It includes splendours of arts of Iranian, Mughal, Central Asian, Kashmiri and Rajasthani schools besides Calligraphic Masterpieces.

Manuscripts

The Library has emerged as an outstanding research Library embracing a large number of rare manuscripts, some of them richly illuminated viz. "Tarik-e-Khandan-e-Timuriya", the only copy in the world, contains 132 beautiful paintings by the famous court artists of Akbar the Great and a writing of Jehangir.

Intellectuals and scholars always speak very high of the Library's precious collection and also acknowledge its prompt services. The reprographic services have been improved with the installation of Minolta Microfilm Reader Printer. In addition to microfilms, xerox copies, slides and photographs, the Library also provides microfilm printouts to researchers on their request. There are a number of manuscripts which are not available in any library of the world.

Cataloguing of manuscripts is one of the major activities of the Library. The Library prepares subjectiwise descriptive catalogues of its manuscripts. The scheme was started by the scholar-administrator Lord Curzon in 1905 ubder the supervision of scholar Sir Denison Ross. So far, 30 volumes of catalogues have been brought out.

Most of the old volumes of catalogues were out of print since long. During the last two decades all the above volumes of old and out-of-print catalogues have been reproduced. Of these some twenty volumes were released with necessary additions and corrections, during the outgoing years. Catalogues of printed books in European Languages in the Library were also released afresh.

The Library is active toward compilation of a union catalogue in order to provide information at one centre, regarding collections of Arabic, Persian and Urdu language manuscripts scattered through out the world. It is making efforts in preparing brief handlist of all such manuscripts which still remain uncatalogued. About a dozen of such collections were covered earlier,

Compilation of descriptive catalogue of manuscripts is also a research work. Our catalogues published so far contain rich information about the manuscripts and hence they are highly valued in the academic world.

The Library has so far published 36 volumes of Descriptive Catalogue of Manuscripts covering about one-third of the total

collection. Moreover, the hand-list of manuscripts in Arabic (3 vols.), Persian (3 vols.) and Urdu (1 vol.) have also been compiled and printed for the benefit of the readers. More volumes of Descriptive Catalogue are likely to be published soon.

Persian Volumes

Poetry (vol. 1)

Poetry (vol.2)

Poetry (volume 3)

Poetry (vol. 6)

Indian History (vol.7)

Biography, Romance, Tales and Anecdotes (col. 8)

Philosophy and Science (vol. 9)

Science and Arts (vol.11)

Commentaries on the Quran, Hadis Law, Theology and Controversial works (vol. 14)

Sufism, Hinduism and the History of Creeds and Sects (vol. 16)

Mixed Contents (vol. 17)

Persian Poetry, History, Biography and Tales (vol. 13)

Encyclopedia of Natural Sciences, Medicine, Logic and Ethics (vol. 13)

Quranic Science Arabic Volumes

Arabic Catalogues

Medical Works (Vol-4)

Tradition (Vol-5)

Theology (Vol-10)

Biography (Vol-12)

Sufism (Vol-13)

History (Vol-15)

Quaranic Science (Vol-18)

Principles of Jurisprudence (Vol-19)

Philology (Vol-20)

Encyclopaedia, Logic, Philosophy and Dialectics (Vol-21)

Science (Vol-22)

Poetry and Elegant Prose (Vol-23)

Ethics and Prayers (Vol-24)

Miscellanies (Vol-25)

Philology (Vol-26)

Miscellanies (Vol-27)

Miscellanies (Vol-28)

Quranic Science (Vol-29)

Tradition (Vol-30)

7
MAULANA AZAD LIBRARY, ALIGARH MUSLIM UNIVERSITY, ALIGARH

The Aligarh Muslim University (AMU), is the most respected and important educational centre for Indian Muslims. It was initially founded as Mohammedan Anglo Oriental College (MAOC) at Aligarh in 1875 by Sir Syed Ahmed Khan (1817-1898) and subsequently raised to the status of Aligarh Muslim University (AMU) in 1920. This University, being the representative body of the upwardly mobile middle class Indian Muslims created a significant impact on Muslim politics in India. The University was the outcome of the Aligarh Movement.

If we look into the historical background of the Aligarh Movement, Sir Syed Ahmed launched it with unique political and educational ideology and objective to restore the lost pride of his community after the fall of Mughals.

From the post of record keeper in East India Company, which Sir Syed had joined in 1837, he rose to the position of Chief Assessment Official in Bijnor at the time of the outbreak of Sepoy mutiny in 1857 (Metcalf). His status in imperial power gradually transformed him to a loyal soldier of British throne. Realising ground political reality with conviction that British rule was to continue for long, he developed his political ideology against the freedom of India from colonial rule and preferred to convince his community to align with the imperial power than to confront with them. Accordingly, he made a tactical move to manage rapport between Muslims and British power by preparing his community as allies to British than their 'subjugation' under Hindu dominated power structures in the country.

It is a known fact of Indian history that Sepoy mutiny of 1857 had made a significant impact on the contemporary social history of this sub-continent. For Muslim elite it caused great mental turmoil as "they were reduced to the position of hewers of woods and drawers of water by the British" (The Aligarh Movement by Dr. Shan Muhammad, 1978, page IX). They took the fall of Mogul Empire as a defeat of the Muslim community.

As a part of his strategy Sir Syed made a sincere attempt to establish a rapport between Muslims and the Government. He issued a series of pamphlets entitled "The loyal Mohammadons of India" in 1860 and tried to dispel the unfavourable impression about Muslims among the British rulers. He also started publishing a journal entitled "Aligarh Institute Gazette" in 1866 and organised a branch of British Indian Association to prove his point. With his write-up on a comparative study of Quran and Bible he tried to convince the Christian rulers that both the Christians and Muslims were friends as both had a common Semitic religious bond.

Sir Syed visited England in 1869 and studied the British system of education and administration. With his sole ambition to transform the Muslim society by harmonizing Islam with western scientific spirit and improving the material prosperity of his community, he renounced the Islamic orthodoxy of Waliullah. His rational interpretation of Islam was however, rejected by his contemporary Muslim clergies as it was contrary to the fundamentalist views on controversial issues like Jihad, polygamy and animal slaughtering. Ultimately, he succumbed to the pressure of fundamentalists and "agreed not to express his views on Islam through his writings" (Rational Approach to Islam by Asghar Ali Engineer – 2001 –page 191).

Contrary to the fundamentalist ideology of Dar-ul-Uloom (abode of Islamic learning) founded in 1866 at Deoband, Sir Syed Ahmad Khan was of the view that backwardness of Muslims could be eradicated only through western education. Accordingly he set up MAO College on his return from England with the help

of British to impart western education along with Islamic knowledge. With his new educational vision he wanted to prepare the Muslim mind to change the failed medieval system of education, which had not met the material and intellectual needs of the community.

The Education Commission of 1882, while lauding the efforts of Sir Syed Ahmed remarked:

"The founders of the institution have realised that the only education which could bring their race into harmony with civilization around them and restore it to a position of influence was an education frankly acknowledging advance of science, catholic in its sympathies with all that was admirable in the literature, history and philosophy of other countries, broad in its outlines and exact in its studies". (History of Aligarh Muslim University, by Khaliq Nizami, page XII).

In spite of his design to resolve the plight of Muslims through western model of education, Sir Syed had to face the challenges of radical Islamists for whom India under British rule was Dar-ul-Harb (Land of war) and Muslims were duty bound to launch jihad (Holy war) against it. In fact the influence of Wahhabi movement and the Islamic thought were so deep in the minds of Muslims that Sir Syed Ahmad Khan failed to generate encouraging urge for modern and scientific education among the members of the community. However, with his missionary zeal he managed the support of a larger section of Muslim elite, who link their personal interest with the larger interest of Indian Muslims.

By rejecting the Indian National Congress Syed further convinced the Muslim elite that in the event of a transfer of power to Indians, it would be handed over to Hindu majority. His preference to Muslim nationalism in comparison to Indian nationalism gradually placed him in a dominant position in the Muslim political scene of North West Provinces and Punjab. Favouring a non-Muslim and non-Hindu rule over India he said, "I have said repeatedly that for India it is impossible that either

Hindus or Muslims are rulers and are able to keep the peace. It is inevitable that a third nation rules over us" Muslim Nationhood in India by Safia Amir – 2000 – page 25). He suggested, "Since the Hindus were joining hands against Muslims (he meant Indian National Congress dominated by Hindus), the latter should unite with the British and strive to make their rule permanent, rather than becoming subjects of the Hindus by joining the Congress" (Ibid page 244).

Muslim elite had no inhibition in adopting western life style despite they spoke of separate Islamic identity. Their pan-Islamic ideology did not allow the concept of a common nationality to emerge against the British. Aligarh movement therefore, made a significant contribution to the unfortunate part of Muslim- Hindu divide. It worked as a catalyst against the unity between Hindus and Muslims to fight against the British. Syed "was largely responsible for keeping away the modern educated Muslims from northern India aloof from Indian National Congress".

The War of Independence 1857 ended in disaster for the Muslims. The British chose to believe that the Muslims were responsible for the anti-British uprising; therefore they made them the subject of ruthless punishments and merciless vengeance. The British had always looked upon the Muslims as their adversaries because they had ousted them from power. With the rebellion of 1857, this feeling was intensified and every attempt was made to ruin and suppress the Muslims forever. Their efforts resulted in the liquidation of the Mughal rule and the Sub-continent came directly under the British crown.

After dislodging the Muslim rulers from the throne, the new rulers, the British, implemented a new educational policy with drastic changes. The policy banned Arabic, Persian and religious education in schools and made English not only the medium of instruction but also the official language in 1835. This spawned a negative attitude amongst the Muslims towards everything modern and western, and a disinclination to make

use of the opportunities available under the new regime. This tendency, had it continued for long, would have proven disastrous for the Muslim community.

Seeing this atmosphere of despair and despondency, Sir Syed launched his attempts to revive the spirit of progress within the Muslim community of India. He was convinced that the Muslims in their attempt to regenerate themselves, had failed to realize the fact that mankind had entered a very important phase of its existence, i.e., an era of science and learning. He knew that the realization of the very fact was the source of progress and prosperity for the British. Therefore, modern education became the pivot of his movement for regeneration of the Indian Muslims. He tried to transform the Muslim outlook from a medieval one to a modern one.

Sir Syed's first and foremost objective was to acquaint the British with the Indian mind; his next goal was to open the minds of his countrymen to European literature, science and technology.

Therefore, in order to attain these goals, Sir Syed launched the Aligarh Movement of which Aligarh was the center. He had two immediate objectives in mind: to remove the state of misunderstanding and tension between the Muslims and the new British government, and to induce them to go after the opportunities available under the new regime without deviating in any way from the fundamentals of their faith.

The establishment of Mohammedan Anglo Oriental (MAO) College in 1875 marks one of the most important events in the educational and social history of modern India. Its establishment is considered as the first significant response of the Indian Muslims to the challenges of post -1857 era. It was an important catalyst in a process of social change among Muslims.

In 1920, an Act of Indian Legislative Council elevated the M.A.O. College to the status of a Central University. Since that time AMU has grown into a major Indian university. It presently covers a very wide spectrum of academic disciplines, having 88 departments, 5 institutions, 13 centres

The University currently has about 28000 students on its rolls, most of whom stay in 16 halls of residences with 70 hostels. It employs about 1400 academic staff, and about 6000 non-teaching staff. On an average, about 500 foreign students come to study at AMU every year. The University has a campus spread over 467.6 hectares of land.

The University Library

The Library complex of the University consists of a Central Library and over 80 college/departmental libraries. Libraries of the colleges, institutes and departments, cater to the needs of postgraduates and students of professional courses.

The University has established Book Banks for the benefit of students of certain professional courses. The Central Library was set up in 1875, when this institution was established as Madarsatul Uloom. In 1877, the Madarsa became Mohammadan Anglo-Oriental College. Lord Lytton, the viceroy of India, laid the foundation stone, and the library was named after him as Lytton Library. Eminent scholars like Gardner Brown, Arnold, Releigh, Horowitz, Storey and Auchtelpone functioned as honorary librarians in addition to their teaching responsibilities.

In 1960, it was named as Maulana Azad Library when the first Prime Minister, Pt. Jawaharlal Nehru, inaugurated its present building. The Seven storied building is surrounded by 4.75 acres of land in the form of beautiful lawns and gardens. It is the most beautiful building of the University and one of the few very attractive libraries in the country. The Library has over 10,00,000 books.

The collection consists of books, periodicals, pamphlets, manuscripts, paintings and photographs. M.A. Library performs the functions of a National Library so far as its collection of Oriental manuscripts are concerned. It is because of these rich collections of immense research value that this Library is reckoned among major libraries of the world. The oldest manuscript owned by the library is more than fourteen hundred

years old. It is a fragment of the Holy Quran transcribed by Hazrat Ali, the fourth caliph of Islam and is written on parchment in *Kufi* script. Another rare collection is the *Halnama* of *Beyazid Ansari*, no copy of which is available anywhere else in the world.

The Library has a sizeable collection of early printed books in various languages. The most outstanding among them is the Latin translation of the celebrated Arabic work on optics, *opticam prafatis,* by Ibn-al-Haitham (965-1039) published in 1572.

There are several *farmans* (decrees) of the Mughal kings like Babur, Akbar, Shahjahan, Shah Alam, Shah Alamgir, Aurangzeb etc. Another prized possession of the library is a "Shirt" on which the whole Quran is inscribed in khafi script. This shirt is believed to have been worn by a warrior of Mughal army.

Among the large collection of Mughal paintings is the painting of Red Blossom, which is magnum opus of Mansoor Naqqash, the celebrated court artist of Emperor Jahangir. Some valuable Sanskrit works translated into Persian have also been preserved in the library. Other possessions worth mentioning is the Ayurved in Telugu and the Bhasa's in Malyalam script written on palm leaves. Abul Faiz Faizi, an eminent scholar of Akbar's court translated several Sanskrit works into Persian, such as Maha Puran, Bhagvat Gita, Mahabharat and Lila Wati, these are also available.

More than 5,000 students, teachers and other members of the university daily visit the library and utilize its services.

Collections of the Library

Sir Syed Ahmad Khan donated his personal collection for the Library at the time of foundation of this university. This library with the other different donated collections was called Lytten Library, after the British Viceroy in India. From 1924 to 1926 Sahibzada Aftab Ahmad Khan was the chancellor of the university. He paid particular attention to the expansion of the library. He also donated his personal collection of rare law books

that he had made while studying at Cambridge University. He allocated a budget for the purchase of useful books for the students. The purchase of these books on different subjects added much to the importance of this library as well as the university. In the same manner, the donation of the valuable personal collections of its professors, nobles and distinguished persons strengthened the scientific work and value of this library In the year 1948 Dr. Zakir Hussain was appointed the vice-chancellor of this university. He paid much attention to this library and felt it necessary to expand the area. and create a more suitable place for keeping the books and better facilities for the students and scholars. For this purpose he prepared the ground so that the chancellor of the university might exchange views with the central goverment and University Grants Commission authorities. He succeeded in obtaining a grant of one million and thirty thousand rupees from central government for the new buildings of the library. Its foundation stone was laid in 1955 by Pandit Jawahar Lal Nehru, the first prime minister of India after the independence of the country. The plan of the new library building, which is considered one of the best specimens of Indo-Islamic architecture, was prepared and carried out by Engineer Fayyaz ud-Din. The new building was inaugurated in 1960. Taking in view the services rendered by Maulana Azad, the great thinker and literacy figure, it was named.

Printed Book Collections

The Aligarh Muslim University library is among the biggest libraries of the country and comes next only to the Delhi University Library from the point of view of the strength of book stock. The library has a total collection of over 10 lacs volumes and 14,571 manuscripts. This vast collection, has certain peculiar features which distinguish it from the collection s of many other libraries of the country. The price less treasure of a large number of manuscripts (some of them very rare and old) covering a wide range of subjects including physical sciences, the enormity and richness of literature in oriental languages, the biggest collection

of Urdu books and periodicals in Asia, the extensive coverage of classical literature in various disciplines, the sizeable volume of publications in many European languages besides English, and the well-rounded collections in various disciplines are some of the striking features of the variegated and rich resources of the library which give it a place of pride not only among libraries within the country but also in the community of world renowned libraries.

Urdu Collection

The Maulana Azad Library posses the largest collection of Urdu books in the Indian sub-continent, which is perhaps the largest in the world as well. It contains over one lakh volumes of publications mostly the out of prints books covering mainly all aspects of Indian life and culture, history, religion, literature, politics, linguistics, literary criticism, Islam and Islamic disciplines and philosophy. There are a large number of books printed in the early 19th century by the Scientific Society of Sir Syed Ahamd Khan, Fort William College Calcutta, Delhi College, Agra College and from the Royal Printing Press of the Courts of Delhi an Oudah. About all important publications of Urdu brought out by the prestigious publishers are available in the Library. Some of the rare publications under this categry include Akhlaq-I-Hind, Araishe Mehfil by Sher Ali Afsos, Baraha Masa by Kazim Ali, Muntakhibat-I-Hindi by John Shakespeare, Jame Jam by Sir Syed Ahmad Khan etc.

Urdu magazine published during the 19th and 20th century form the most significant part of the Urdu Collection. They include Akhbar Scientific Society, Tehzibul Akh;laq (Aligarh. 1879), Punjab Review etc. The periodicals published in the 20th Century which are available in the Library include Makhzan (Lahore 1901), Zamana (Kanour, 1903) Urdu-e-Mualla (Aligarh 1903), Ismat (Delhi, 1908). Oriental College Magazine (Lahore, 1925) etc.

Urdu Collection of the Library has been enriched by a

number of eminent personalities in literature by their donations of invaluable books. Some of the most famous among such collections are Dr. Ram Babu Saxena, Subhanullah, Adbus Salam, Habibganj etc. The University Library has acquired the personal library of the renowned scholar, Maulana Abdul Majd Daryabadi comprising about 4000 books and back volumes of journals and also the personal collection of the renowned Urdu poet Kaifi Azmi recently.

Arabic Collection

The Arabic collection of Maulana Azad Library contains about 30,000 volumes. The subject covered in the Arabic collection include Muslim Philosophy, Mysticism, Quranic studies, Hadith and Physical sciences, Arabic Poetry and literature and history. Reference sources in Arabic are also available covering the Medieval as well as modern literature. Noticeable among the holdings are the Quanoon of Avicenna (Rome, 1593), Nazamul Jawahar of Ibn Bitreeq (Oxonia, 1654), Historia Orientalis (1660) Bible in Arabic and Latin (Rome 1671) etc.

Persian Collection

The Persian collection comprises of about 18000 volumes which are a valuable reference sources on Medieval Indian History. It also includes rich literature of India and Iran in Persian language. The other subjects covered by the Persian collection mainly include History of Islam, Indian Sciences, Mathematics, Unani System of Medicine etc. There are some early printed and rare books such as Hidaya; translated by Ghulam Yahya Khan (1807), Uruz Saifi (1872), Diwan-e-Saeb (1853) Anwar Sahili bu Mulla Husain Kashifi (1816) Marat-I-Daulat-I-Abbasiya by Daulat Rai (1850) Zafar Nama by Hatfi Abdullah (1869) etc. Another significant holding of the Library is the Shah Nama of Firdausi which was received as a gift from the Iranian Embassy.

Sanskrit Collection

Sanskrit was introduced as a subject of study in the University from the very beginning. Therefore, a fine collection

of Sanskrit books has been developed over the years. The Sanskrit collection now includes about 6,500 volumes. Almost all the important and famous publications have found place in this collection. Some of them are; Leelavati (Calcutta, 1846) Upanishad with the commentrary of Shankar Acharya (Calcutta, 1873) and Pawan Dootam) (1873.

Hindi Collection

The Hindi collection comprises of about 35,000 volumes. Special feture of the collection is that it holds about all Hindi translations of classical Urdu literature. Diwan-e-Ghalib and Deewan-e-Mir can be cited in this context. Special attention has been paid to procure historical sources of Medieval period which have been translated into Hindi.There are some rare and out of print books also. Besides Hindi, the Library holds books in other Indian languages like Tamil, Telugu, Malayalam, Bengali, Marathi, Kashmiri, Dogri etc.

Sir Syed Collection

Sir Syed is not only the founder of the Aligarh Muslim University but also a great literary figure and a social thinker of India. All his works and also the literature on him has been arranged separately to facilitate the researchers. The collection also contains the files of famous Aligarh Institute Gazette and Tehzibul Akhlaq, started by Sir Syed. The collection has great value for the researchers on political, social and educational history of Indian Muslims.

Gandhian Collection

Gandhian Collection contains books written by and on Gandhiji on diverse subjects including all the collected works of Gandhiji published by the Publications Division of the Govt. of India. The collection also includes the works of celebrated authors like C.F. Andrews, R. R. Diwaker, Madhav Desai, Louis Fischer, Acharya Kirplani, Jawaharlal Nehru, Peyarelal, Radhakrishnan and a number of foreign writers. The collection includes

publications in English, Urdu and Hindi and their translations from one language to the other. These books are displayed in the Library on the occasion of Gandhi Jayanti.

Aligarh Collection

This collection provides basic source material on the growth of the Aligarh Muslim University from the very beginning. It contains both official and semi-official publications of the institution. Besides containing the reports of different committees on raising the M A O College into the University, the collection includes annual reports and the minutes of the bodies like University Court, Executive Council and Academic Councils etc. The departmental reports, enquiry committee reports, halls magazines, inaugral addresses and records of academic activities of the University are also included in this collection.

Thesis Collection

The thesis collection comprises of theses and dissertations of Ph. D., D. Lit., D. Sc., and also the dissertations of postgraduate courses. It includes all thesis and dissertations submitted to the University irrespective of their languages.

Archives

This collection is important for the purpose of serious research since the archival records of the University dating back to 1963 which run into several hundred thousand are kept there.

Microfiches

This collection is based on about 30,000 microfiches containg 1,25,000 pages of rare materials. The noticeable item include Census of India from 1872 to 1951, India Registers (India Office list) covering the period 1717 till independence, selection from dispatches to the Govt. of India for the period 1858-1936 and also valuable journals published during the 18th and 19th centuries.

Manuscripts Collection

The manuscripts collection is the most prestigious and invaluable collection of the Library. This collection also originated from the personal library of Sir Syed Ahmed Khan who had a great passion for collecting manusscripts. The copy of the manuscript 'Tarikh-e-Gazida' which contains notes of the famous scholar, Abul Faiz Faizi, is infact from the founders's own collection. This collection is on of the largest on the sub continents is known is to scholars throughout the academic world. Some of its highly important and rare manuscripts have attracted the attention of renowned orientalists who have listed them in their monumental bibliographical surveys (1), Geschicte der Arabischen Litterutur (GDAL) by Carl Brocklemann; (2) Geschicte das Arabischen Schrifttums (GDAS) by Fuat Sezgin and (3) Persian Literature: a bibliographical survey by C .A. Storey.

The collection contains source material on a variety of subjects. Its coverage is very wide and extends to numerous fields of human knowledge which may briefly be assumed up as under:-

1. Islamic theology; the holy Quran and its commentaries; Hadith (traditions); fiqh and usul-i-fiqh (muslim jurisprudence), aqaid; translations of other holy scriptures.
2. Sufic literature.
3. Philosphy: logic; metaphysics; ethics; dogmatics philosophy (Ilmul kalam).
4. History: general history of the world ; history of different regions; history of India-Sultanate period, Mughal and Mugal period' bibliographies.
5. Literature: prose and belles letters; poetry-epic, didactic, collective works of poets.
6. Linguistics: dictionaries, grammer (sarf and nahv); rhetoric and prosody (banyan, and, arud).
7. Geography and travelogues.

8. Exact sciences; mathmatics; astronomy; chemisty and mineralogy; botany; zoology; agriculture, medicine and veterinary science.
9. Pseudo sciences: astrology sciences: astrology; geomancy; divination; interpretation of dreams;
10. Encyclopaedic works.
11. Varia; music; hunting; calligraphy; art of war,etc.
12. Translation of Sanskrit works into Persian.

This magnificent and priceless collection has been built up over a period of more than a century. According to a report the total number of manuscripts in 1924 was just 628. Today it stands at well over 14,500. The language wise breake –up of the collection is as follows:-

(a)	Arabic	5107
(b)	Persian	8255
(c)	Urdu	1075
(d)	Hindi	116
(e)	Sanskrit	3

In its evolutionary growth the collection is heavily indebted to the munificence of great scholars and bibliophiles who donated their entire personal libraries to the university. There are eleven such donations which are named after the names of their respective donors. The university has also purchased from its own resources a few thousand manuscripts. The respective strength of the different constituents of the manuscripts collection:

1.	Subhanullah Collection	2,399
2.	Habibganj Collection	1,616
3.	Abdus Salam Collection	575
4.	Firangi Mahal Collection	1,552
5.	Sulaiman Collection	1,412
6.	Qutubuddin Collection	235

8.	Mmunir Alam Collection	117
9.	Aftab Collection	353
10.	Ahsan Collection	353
10.	Shaifta Collection	209
11.	Jawahar Museum (Etawah) collection	1,643
12.	University collection	4,330

Of these collection, the Subhanullah collection is not only the largest but also the richest so far as the subject coverage is concerned. The collection is also known for its illuminated manuscripts and fine art of calligraphy.

The Habib Ganj collection is another treasure of immense academic and research value which has enormously enriched the manuscripts resources of the Library. The collection forms part of the library of the late Nawab Sardar Yar Jung Bahadur Habibur Rehman Khan Sherwani saheb. Sherwani Saheb had built up an impressive library of manuscripts and printed books. After his death his illustrious son, Khan Bahadur Haji Obaidur Rehman Khan Sherwani saheb, whose association with the university spreads over several decades and who also has held the office of the vice chancellor of this University more than once, made a gift of the Habibganj library to the university library. This collection is very rich in literature on Islamics, mysticism, Persian period. It includes substantial paintings of the Mughal period and very beautiful front pieces and embellished borders.

The catalogue of the Persian poetry manuscripts of this collection has been published. In this catalouge Mathnavi Ma'navi, Bostan-e-S, adi, Diwan-e-Asif Mazhar-al- Asrar Diwan-e-Rozbhan Sabri, Kulliyat-e-Urfi, Diwan-e Hafiz, Qasaed-e-Faizi, Diwan-e-Saeb, Majm,ul Bahrain, Diwan-e-Ibne Yamin, Diwan-e-Amir Shahi, Diwan-e-Bedil, Kulliyat-e-Hazin, Diwan-e-Kamal Khujandi, Saulate-e-Usmania, etc., are very important for more than one reason. Some are quite rare and no copy thereof is available anywhere in the world . Some had been on the shelves

of royal libraries and bear the seal or contain notes of the kings and nobles whom they once belonged to. Still others have been copied out by famous calligraphists.

From the point of view of the historical significance the university collection and the Abdussalam collection are very important . These collections bristle with original source material in the history of Afghan rule in India and the Medieval Indian history . The Habibganj, Subhanullah, Shaifta Sulaiman and Munir Alam collections also contain quite a good number of manuscripts on history. Some of the important manuscripts of this category are Subh-e-Sadiq by Mirza Momohammad Sadiq Sadiqui bin Mohammad Sualeh Asfahani (d.1651), Mirat-e- Aftab Numa by Abdur Rehman (1217A.H.), Haqiqat-hai Hindustan by Lachmi Narain Shafiq (1204A.H.), Zikrul Muluk by Shaikh Abdul Haq Muhaddis Dehlavi (1030A.H.), Tarikh-e-Tabri translated by Abu Muhammad 1029-30A.H.), Tazkrat-us-Salatin-e-Chighta by Mohammad Hadi (1132A.H.) and Tawarikh-e-Azizi by Shah Abdul Aziz Dehlavi.

The oldest manuscripts owned by the library is a fragment of the holy Quran consisting of Surah Fateha and a portion of Surah Baqrah. It is written on parchment in Kufic script and is believed to have been transcribed by Hazrat Ali, the fourth caliph of Islam. There is another copy of Quran which, it is said, is the handiwork of emperor Aurangzeb. Yet another copy of the holy book is the original work of Haddad the famous calligraphist in the court of Shahjahan. The particular feature of one more Quranic manuscript is that it contains only thirty pages and each page contains one chapter (parah) of the book note with standing the fact that all the chapters vary length. Besides these copies there is large no of magnificently illuminated copies of the Quran, some of which belonged to the imperial collections of the great Mughals. Othere manuscripts of the Quran are fine specimen of calligraphy. There are some curious besides manuscripts, e.g. a shirt on which the whole Quran is inscribed. According to the annual report of the university for the year 1933, the shirt was

recieved as a gift by Sir Ross Masood, the then vice chancellor, from his friend, lord Lothian

A number of manuscripts are pretty old and some of them date back as early as the 5th and 6th century A.H./11th and 12th century and quite a few are so rare that no copy thereof is traceable in any other library of the world. Some example are given below:-

1. Autograph copy of 'Uyunul ajwabah fi fanuni laswalah' by the renowned mystic Al-Qushairi (A. H.1072).
2. Nihjul-balaghah in two volumes transcribed in 538 A.H. It is surly the earlest Muslim work on the administration of government and contains the dicourses and instructions issued from time to time to his governors by Hazrat Ali. Compiled by Sharif al-Razi d.406 A. H../1015 A. D. It is considered to be the oldest second copy of the manuscript available in the world.
3. Hal Namah of Bayazid Ansari which contains a short biography of the famous saint Bayazid Ansari of Akbar's period as also a succint account of Roshana'iyah movement down to the reign of Shah Jahan. It was compiled by Ali Mohammed bin Abu Bakr Qandhari. No other copy of this manuscript is available anywhere in the world.
4. Jamharat –o-ash,ar,il Arab, compiled by Abul Khattab al-Qarshi is a compilation of Arabic poetry which was transcribed in 998 A.H. No other copy older than this is traceable.
5. Nafais-ul-Ma'sir by Mirza Alauddulah Nami Qazwaini 1565-1571 A.D. which contains an account of the poets of the 10th century A.H. and the history of Mughals from Babar to Akbar is also known for its rarity. Only a few extracts from this mss. are available in the British Museum.
6. Autograph copy of al-Jami,us Sahih by Ibn-l-Hajr as-Saqalan 852 A. H. /1448 A.D.
7. Madanul- Jawahar by Waliullah Frangi Mahli d.1127 A.D. /1853 A.D. is a voluminous commentary on the holy Quran.

It is also a unique mss. as no other copy is available elsewhere.

8. Tafsir-e-Yaqub Charkhi is another commentary on the Holy Quran very few copies of which are available only in some European libraries.

Some of the manuscripts have the peculiarity of being transcribed by the authors themselves such manuscripts include Diwan-e-Saeb fat hulmut al fi madhulan al by Ahmad bin Mohammad al Maghrabi 1033 A.H.. Khutbatul Qawaid by Fakhruddin bin Mohammad al–Hasan bin Yusuf Ali bin al-Muthar 900 A.H. etc. There is also one more copy of Diwan-e-Saeb which was transcribed by his disciple, Arif Tabraizi in 1085 A.H. This copy was gone through by Saeb as is evident from the additions made by him of some of his ghazals on the margin of different pages.

Several manuscripts stand out distinctly because of being profusely illustrated and studded with very fine miniature paintings . Khamsa-i-Nizami by Nizami Ganjivi transcribed by Husain Abdulla in 873 A.H.Mathnavi Husaini 1163 A. H.Diwan-e-Hafiz transcribed by Abdul Rehman in 971 A.H. Mathnavi Maulvi M,navi transcribed by Abdullah bin Qambar Samarkhandi in1019 A.D. and Hamla-i-Haideri by Mohammad Rafi Khan Mashhadi deserve special mention.

Among the illuminated manuscripts is Karima transcribed by Badar Ali in 1277 A.H. Mulfuzat saheb qiran by Afzal Bukhari and transcribed by Hidayatullah in 1220 A.H. Haft band kashi transcribed by Atarud Raqam in 1280 A.H. and Qasidah dar manqabat Hazrat Ali provide a fine feast for the eyes.

The collection also contains a substantial number of manuscripts which are beautifully transcribed in this context Diwan-e-Lisani transcribed by Hasan Quli in 983 A.H. Khamsa–i-Nizami transcribed by Firoz Mohammad bin Sulaiman in Nastaliq script, Mathnavi Maulana Rum 1089 A.H. and Tabaqat-i-Akbari by Khwaja Nizamuddin Bakhshi transcribed by Abdul

Haq Qureshi in 1003 A.H. may be cited as just a few examples.

The collection is rich in the works of Persian translations. Most of the Sanskrit epics including Mahabharat renderd into Persian by Naqib Khan who was one of the prominent nobles of Emperor. Akbar. Abul Fazal Faizi translated Maha Purana, Bhagvat Gita, Ramayana, Mahabharata, and Lilavati into Persian. Dara Shikoh was also a Persian scholar who translated Jog Vashistht and Upanishad into Persian. Besides these works, Persian translation of several Sanskrit works like Hitpdesha entitled Mufarrihul Qulub by Taj Mufti-al- Makki etc are also available in the Library.

The Manuscript Division of the Library also possess several farmans (edicts) of the Mughal Kings. The largest among them is the farman issued by Babar under his own seal. It is the only farman of Babar in existence. The Division also contains about a thousand coins mostly belonging to the Medieval Indian period. Besides this, the Division has some rare paintings, and rotographs and autographed letters from eminent personalities.

The catalogues of some collections have also been published. They include :

1. **Habib Ganj Collection:** This collection was donated by Ubaidur Rahman Khan Sherwani son of Nawwab Sadr Yar Jang Habibur Rahman Sherwani (1867-1950 A.D.) to the university in the year 1960. The catalogue of 813 manuscripts in Arabic, Persian and Urdu has been published in three volumes so far.

2. **Ahsan Marehravi Collection (1876-1940 A.D.):** Maulana Ahsan Marehravi was one of the professors of Urdu at Aligarh Muslim University. He taught this language from 1922 to 1940. He compiled his political works in two volumes, namely Faiz-e Dagh and Mohavarat. His collection consists of fine and rare printed and unpublished books in Arabic, Hindi, Persian and Urdu. It consists of about 350 volumes.

3. Jawahar Museum Collection : This catalogue has been compiled by Mohammad Abrar Husain Farooqi and published in 1959. It describes 182 Persian manuscripts of Jawahar Museum, Itawa.

4. **Shaifta Collection:** The collection was donated by Nawwab Mohammad Mustafa Khan Shaifta (1802-1869 A.D.). In 1982 the catalogue of Shaiftah Collection manuscripts was prepared and printed by Sayyed Mahmud Hasan Qaisar Amrohavi. This catalogue includes the description of about 200 volumes of the Shaifta Collection.

5. **Aftab Collection :** This collection comprises of 66 Arabic, 162 Persian and 3 Urdu manuscripts. Its catalogue was compiled by Mohd. Hasan Rizvi and Syed Mehmood Husain Daisar.

6. **Subhanullah Collection :** The catalogue of this collection was compiled by Syed Kamil Husain and published in 1930.

7. **Mirat-al-Tasawwuf :** It consists of manuscripts on Sufism. The catalogue of this collection was compiled by syed Mohammad Hasan Qaisar in 1980.

8

HAKIM MOHAMMAD SAID LIBRARY, JAMIA HAMDARD, NEW DELHI

The history of Jamia Hamdard begins with the establishment of a small Unani clinic in the year 1906 by Hakeem Hafiz Abdul Majeed, one of the well-known practitioners of Unani System of Medicine of his time. Hakeem Hafiz Abdul Majeed had a vision of making the practice of Unani Medicine into a scientific discipline so that Unani medicines could be dispensed in a more efficacious manner to patients. He gave the name "Hamdard" to his venture which means "sympathy for all and sharing of pain". His illustrious son, Hakeem Abdul Hameed, carried forward the philosophy and objectives of Hamdard in independent India. Even at the time of partition of India in 1947, Hakeem Abdul Hameed was dreaming of setting up a complex of educational institutions which would concentrate on highlighting the contribution of Islam and Islamic culture to Indian civilization and development of Unani medicines for curing diseases.

On th 28th August, 1948, Hamdard, which was a commercial enterprise at that time, was converted into a Wakf, with the object of giving effect to Islamic teachings of public charity including health and education. In 1964, Hamdard National Foundation was created with a view to receive and disburse the profits earned by Hamdard (Wakf) Laboratories. Hamdard National Foundation was to take up charitable causes in the areas of education, medical relief and the advancement of knowledge, consistent with the principles of the true teachings of Islam.

For setting up a complex of research and educational institutions, Hakeem Abdul Hameed purchased a piece of land in Tughlaqabad area of South Delhi which was hardly inhabited in those times. In order to implement and execute the objects of Wakf as enshrined in the Wakf deed, Hakeem Abdul Hameed and his Muslim associates, established several institutions for teaching and research.

In 1962, Hakeem Abdul Hameed set up the Institute of History of Medicine and Medical Research with the object of promoting education and research in the history of medicine, besides appraising the principles of medicine.

In 1963, Hakeem Abdul Hameed and his Muslim friends and associates set up Indian Institute of Islamic Studies with a view to promote the study of Islamic Culture and Civilization especially its contribution to Indian society and culture.

In 1963, Hamdard Tibbi College was set up in Gali Qasim Jaan, Old Delhi. It was later shifted to Jamia Hamdard Campus in 1980 to provide education in Unani Medicine to students so that the heritage of Unani Medicine largely available in Arabic and Persian is passed on to the students of next generation.

In 1972, Hamdard College of Pharmacy was set up with the objective of providing education and training in all branches of pharmacy. The year 1989 saw the fulfilment of the dream of Hakeem Abdul Hameed when Jamia Hamdard was given the status of Deemed to be University by the Ministry of Human Resource Development on 10th May, 1989. All the above named institutions set up by Hakeem Abdul Hameed and his friends and associates were amalgamated into Jamia Hamdard. In a brief period of only ten years, Jamia Hamdard has evolved into an institution fulfilling the objects of the wakf, which has funded it.

It was a day of great joy for Hakeem Abdul Hameed, founder and the moving spirit behind all the institutions promoted by Hamdard and his large number of friends and associates. As a means of thanking the Almighty for His guidance to its founder

and his associates, Jamia Hamdard adopted a Seal with an ayat from Sura al-Jum'a from the Holy Quran

This verse is translated as under: "he (The Prophet, may peace be upon him) instructs them in `the Book And Wisdom'. Since the founding of Jamia Hamdard, this ayat from the Holy Quran is a source of inspiration and guidance for those connected with Jamia Hamdard management and administration. Jamia Hamdard was inaugurated by Late Shri Rajiv Gandhi on August 01, 1989. In his impressive speech, the Prime Minister lauded the efforts of Hakeem Abdul Hameed in setting up institutions of learning which were emerging in the form of a "Deemed to be University". He said, "This will enable (the Muslim) minority to go forward and help India to march forward". Contribution of Hakeem Abdul Hameed to promote the cause of education, health and social service was acknowledged by the Government of India in 1965 when he was awarded Padma Shri for his valuable contribution and for his personal qualities of sacrifice, devotion and commitment to the cause of education. He was also awarded the Padma Bhushan in 1991. The services rendered by Hakeem Abdul Hameed to the cause of education of Muslims have been acknowledged not only in India but in other countries too. Jamia Hamdard was conceived as a seat of higher learning in Unani Medicine, Islamic Studies, Biosciences, Pharmacy, Nursing and other areas of knowledge by its founder as a means of fulfilling the objects of the wakf. Over a period of last ten years, Jamia Hamdard has emerged as an outstanding institution of higher learning with distinct and focused academic programmes. Graduate programme in Information Technology and Computer Applications and Post-graduate programmes in Information Technology, Computer Applications, Business Management, Physiotherapy and Occupational Therapy have been started in the last few years. Undergraduate programmes in Physiotherapy and Occupational Therapy are being introduced from this year. Jamia Hamdard offers postgraduate and doctoral programmes in several disciplines for which advanced facilities are available.

Hakim Mohammed Said Central Library

Library Collections

I. Conventional Collection

The total library holdings exceed 1.46 lakh including 1,05,000 English, Urdu, Arabic, Persian, Hindi, etc. books. 17,000 bound volumes, 20,000 rare collections and 4500 manuscripts, mostly in Urdu, Arabic and Persian languages. The library receives 200 Indian and foreign journals, out of which 124 by subscriptions and 76 by gratis, covering medicine, pharmacy, nursing, biotechnology, toxicology, computer science, management science, religion and social sciences

II. Special Collections

The library has some special collections:

i. Naziria collection,

ii. Abdul Sattar Siddiqui collection,

iii. Maulana Abdul Salam Niazi collection,

iv. Jaffri collection,

v. Shafi Ahmad collection

vi. Dr Tanveer Alvi collection

Nearly, 90% of these collections are in Urdu, Arabic and Persian languages, and the remaining 10% are in English, Hindi and Sanskrit languages. Most of these books are very old and information contain in these books are extremely valuable as these are not available in almost all Indian and foreign libraries and are the scholarly contributions of many scholars and academicians of bygone days. Main themes of most of the books are on Islam and its multi-dimensional influences on different religions worldwide.

Research scholars, academicians, etc., specially in the field of Islamic studies may be highly benefited by studying these valuable resources available in Jamia Hamdard Central library.

III. Press Clippings

The library has nearly 2,50,000 press clippings built up since 1964. These are systematically arranged under 500 subject headings as selected by the Late Hakeem Abdul Hamid, the founder of the university.

IV. Non-Conventional Collection

There are 237 microfilm rolls, covering 940 very rare manuscripts, 700 microfiche, 2 CD-ROMs databases –MEDLINE and TOXLINE, and huge collections of CDs, covering computer science and related fields.

Special Sections

Besides plethora of invaluable resources properly organised and managed in different sections of the Hamdard library, it has two very special sections—i. Manuscript and ii. Museum, which need little elaboration by virtue of their rare knowledge bases for in depth study by research scholars and academicians interested in different fields of human knowledge.

Manuscripts

The central library has about 4500 rare manuscripts, having great research value and these are mostly in Urdu, Arabic and Persian languages. These deal with almost all important areas in the field of Islamic Studies, Medicines and different branches of sciences. Most of these manuscripts are handwritten by the authors. Scholars can consult these manuscripts in the section in presence of the In-charge of the section. Manuscripts which are in microfilm forms could be consulted with the help of the Micro-film readers available in the Reprographic section. Printed catalogues of manuscripts of different libraries in India are available for consultation in the section.

Museum

The museum is housed on the ground floor of the central library building. It comprises sculptures, glass and porcelain exhibits, instruments, documentary material, charts, diagrams,

etc., giving a comprehensive idea of the evolution of medicine from the pre-historic and proto-historic times to the modern world. It has three fold purposes. It helps: (a) in teaching of science and culture, (b) in tracing the history of development of medicine, and (c) in assisting research scholars. The display covers all great civilizations of the world and helps both medical students and laymen to grasp the amazing dimensions of science and art of healing. A restoration laboratory and a mounting unit are attached to the museum. It is planned to add many new artifacts and museum specimens to make this facility a more useful source of reference and knowledge.

Library had completed its first phase of automation on receipt of the grants-in –aid of Rs.6.50 lakh from UGC during the year 1999-2000. It had completed the installation of Local Area Network (LAN) having 21 terminals, scattered in four floors of the library building. It had also completed catalogue databases for books, serials and theses/dissertations by using CDS/ISIS (3.08) package on receipt of the recurring grants-in-aid of Rs.1.17 lakh during 2000-2001.

As library has huge collections of Urdu, Arabic, Persian, etc. books, it purchased a software INPAGE for preparing catalogues of these books. So far, more than 5000 records had been completed and it has facilitated searching of books by author, title and keyword.

Library has planned to purchase LIBSYS software very soon and all the records of books, serials and theses/dissertations in English language will be loaded to this user-friendly package. As the software has all the required modules for almost all the activities of the library it will be possible to automate all the sections of the library and also it will accelerate in providing all possible services to user community.

9

DR. ZAKIR HUSAIN LIBRARY, JAMIA MILLIA ISLAMIA, NEW DELHI

Jamia Millia Islamia, an institution originally established at Aligarh in United Provinces, India in 1920 became a Central University by an act of the Indian Parliament in 1988. In Urdu language, Jamia means 'University', and Millia means 'National'.

The story of its growth from a small institution in the pre-independence India to a central university located in New Delhi—offering integrated education from nursery to research in specialized areas—is a saga of dedication, conviction and vision of a people who worked against all odds and saw it growing step by step. They "built up the Jamia Millia stone by stone and sacrifice by sacrifice," said Sarojini Naidu, the nightingale of India.

Under the colonial British rule, two dominant trends joined hands and contributed towards in the birth of Jamia. One was the anti-colonial Islamic activism and the other was the pro-independence aspiration of the politically radical section of western educated Indian Muslim intelligentsia. In the political climate of 1920, the two trends gravitated together with Mahatma Gandhi as a catalyst. The anti-colonial activism signified by the Khilafat and the pro-independence aspirations symbolised by the non-cooperation movement of the Indian National Congress helped to harness creative energies and the subsequent making of Jamia Millia Islamia. Rabindranath Tagore called it "one of the most progressive educational institutions of India".

Responding to Gandhiji's call to boycott all educational institutions supported or run by the colonial regime, a group of

nationalist teachers and students quit Aligarh Muslim University, protesting against its pro-British inclinations. The prominent members of this movement were Maulana Mahmud Hasan, Maulana Mohamed Ali, Hakim Ajmal Khan, Dr. Mukhtar Ahmad Ansari, and Abdul Majid Khwaja.

Born out of political crisis, it seemed for a while, Jamia would not survive the heat of the intense political struggle for the independence of India. It participated in the Bardoli resolution and sent volunteers across the country to motivate people to fight for the freedom of the country. The colonial British government soon imprisoned many of its teachers and students. In 1922, Gandhiji called off the non-cooperation movement. Even as its teachers and students were being released, Mustapha Kemal Ataturk declared the end of the Khilafat in 1924.

Suddenly Jamia saw itself in a great crisis. Some thought it had achieved its mission, as others believed that the institution had lost its raison d'etre with the end of the non-cooperation and the Khilafat movements. Even the little financial assistance, that the Khilafat had been giving it, also dried up. As even prominent people started deserting it, Jamia's total collapse virtually became an imminent possibility.

The saying, 'when going gets tough the tough gets going' cannot be truer about Jamia. As the crisis loomed large, Hakim Ajmal Khan, Dr. Mukhtar Ahmed Ansari and Abdul Majeed Khwaja—the first trio—supported by Gandhiji shifted Jamia from Aligarh to Karol Bagh, in New Delhi in 1925. Gandhiji boosted the morale of Jamia, saying, "The Jamia has to run. If you are worried about its finances, I will go about with a begging bowl". Jamia followed Gandhiji's constructive programme for self-reliance while it took to Charkha and Takli as favoured vocations.

Although Gandhi's contacts helped to secure financial help for Jamia, the risk of helping a Congress-backed institution under the British Raj dissuaded many willing benefactors. Orthodox Muslims also viewed Jamia as a threat to Aligarh Muslim University, the 'Muslim Oxford'. During those difficult days, it

was Hakim Ajmal Khan who met most of Jamia's expenses from his own pocket. Dr. M.A. Ansari and Abdul Majeed Khwaja toured India and abroad, explaining the importance of Jamia and collecting funds for this noble enterprise. Their collective intervention did avert a collapse that was almost certain.

In 1925, after long deliberation, a group of three friends studying in Germany—Dr. Zakir Husain, Dr. Abid Husain and Dr. Mohammad Mujeeb—decided to serve Jamia. Dr. Zakir Husain, who had earned his doctorate in Economics from the University of Berlin, was a natural and charismatic leader. Dr. Abid Husain had his Ph.D. in Education. Mohammad Mujeeb, an Oxford scholar in History and a student of printing in Germany, was a passionate and committed reformist. Early in February 1926, the three friends left Germany for Jamia by the Norddeutscher Lloyd steamer, SS Derfflinger.

In Jamia, Dr. Zakir Husain, was offered a salary of Rs. 100. His two other friends with European qualifications were offered Rs 300 each. Realising that the possibility of making payments was beyond Jamia's limited resources, Abid Husain and Mohammad Mujeeb voluntarily reduced their salaries to Rs. 100 each. Moved by the commitment of his friends, Dr. Zakir Husain also reduced his own salary to Rs. 80. One of the first steps they took was the introduction of the hugely popular evening classes for adult education. This movement was later to become, in October 1938, an institution called Idara-i-Taleem-o-Taraqqi. It kept growing so popular that separate rooms had to be built to accommodate the students.

In 1928 Hakim Ajmal Khan passed away. That was the beginning of the second financial crisis, as it was Hakim Sahib himself who had been meeting most of Jamia's financial needs. The leadership of Jamia then moved into the hands of Dr. Zakir Husain, who became its Vice Chancellor in 1928. To resolve Jamia of these frequent crises, a group of young Jamia teachers, led by Dr. Zakir Husain, took a pledge to serve Jamia for the next twenty years on a salary not more than Rs. 150. This group

was called the Life Members of Jamia. (History repeated in 1942 when a second group of Jamia teachers took a similar pledge).

Jamia's department of Printing and Publications was trifurcated in 1928 with the newly established Jamia Press at Darya Ganj, Urdu Academy, and Maktaba Jamia under the charge of Prof. Mohammad Mujeeb, Dr. Abid Husain and Mr. Hamid Ali respectively.

On 1 March 1935, the foundation stone for a school building was laid at Okhla, then a non-descript village in the southern outskirts of Delhi. In 1936, all institutions of Jamia, except Jamia Press, the Maktaba and the library, were shifted to the new campus. The basic emphasis of Jamia was on evolving innovative education methods. This led to the establishment of a teacher's college (Ustadon ka Madrasa) in 1938. In 1936, Dr. M.A. Ansari passed away. On 4 June 1939, Jamia Millia Islamia was registered as a society.

The fame of Jamia as an innovative education movement spread and dignitaries from foreign countries began visiting Jamia. Husein Raouf Bey (1933), Dr. Behadjet Wahbi of Cairo (1934), Ms. Halide Edib of Turkey (1936) were some of them. Foreigners, impressed by Jamia, began working in Jamia. The German lady Ms. Gerda Philipsborn (popularly known as Aapa Jaan) served Jamia for many years is buried in Jamia.

In 1939, Maulana Ubaidullah Sindhi (1872-1944), a theologian and freedom fighter, came to stay in Jamia on the invitation of Dr. Zakir Husain. He started a school of Islamic Studies in Jamia, called Baitul Hikmal, propagating the ideology of Shah Waliullah. Zakir Husain, later the President of India, recalled those days of indestructible optimism in the face of depravity 'when they had a longing to build and nothing to build with, as "days of joy".

In 1946, during Jamia's silver jubilee celebration, one could see the crisis that India had to face in the following year: Mr. and Mrs. Mohammad Ali Jinnah, and Liyaqat Ali Khan were

on one side of Dr. Zakir Husain, the vice chancellor, on the dias; Pandit Jawaharlal Nehru, Asaf Ali and Sir C Rajagolapachari were on the other side.

The riots following partition that shook the northern India did affect Jamia; but not its campus. Gandhi observed that its campus remained "an oasis of peace in the Sahara" of communal violence. Maktaba Jamia alone lost books worth seven lakhs in arson.

After the attainment of Independence, Jamia continued to grow as an academic institution with a difference. Many foreign dignitaries made it a point to visit Jamia Millia Islamia during their visits to New Delhi. Among those who visited Jamia include Marshal Tito (1954), king Zahir Shah of Afghanistan (1955), crown prince Faisal of Saudi Arabia, king Reza Shah Pehlavi of Iran (1956) and prince Mukarram Jah (1960).

Following the death of Mr. Abdul Majeed Khwaja in 1962, Dr. Zakir Husain, who by then had taken charge as the Vice President of India, became Jamia's Chancellor (1963).

Deemed to be University

In 1962, the University Grants Commission declared the Jamia a 'deemed to be University'. Soon thereafter, the School of Social Work was established in 1967. In 1971, Jamia started the Zakir Husain Institute of Islamic Studies, to honour Dr. Zakir Husain, who had passed away in 1969. BE course in Civil Engineering commenced in 1978; in 1981, the faculties of Humanities and Languages, Natural Sciences, Social Science, and the State Resource Centre were founded. In 1983, it started the Mass Communication Research Centre and the Centre for Coaching and Career Planning. In 1985, it established the Faculty of Engineering & Technology and the University Computer Centre. Academic Staff College and the Academy of Third World Studies followed in 1987 and 1988.

Central University

By a Special Act of the Parliament, Jamia Millia Islamia

was made a central university of India in December 1988. In the list of the Faculties, i.e. Education, Humanities & Languages, Natural Sciences, Social Sciences. Engineering & Technology, one more Faculty - Faculty of Law, was added in 1989. Many new courses and programmes at UG and PG levels have since been added.

Besides its six faculties, the Jamia has a number of centres of learning and research, like Mass Communication Research Centre (MCRC), Academy of Third World Studies (ATWS) etc. The Jamia is also marching ahead in the field of Information Technology (IT). It offers various undergraduate and postgraduate IT courses. Apart from this, the Jamia has a campus wide network which connects a large number of its departments and offices.

About the Library

Dr Zakir Husain Library named after the President of India Late Dr. Zakir Husain in 1973, is the Central Library of the Jamia Library System, which includes the Faculty and Center libraries. Stocking a rich collection of over 3.00 Lacs learning resources in all major discipline taught in the University and spread over an area of 23,038 sq. feet, the library caters to the academic need of the University students, staff & research scholars. It has two spacious reading rooms of 1800 sq. feet each. The collection consists of books, periodicals, pamphlets, manuscripts and photographs. The stack rooms which consist of ground floor plus three upper stories have a carpet area of 9000 sq. feet besides these two halls of same area each house reference and the rare book collection. Periodical section is of 11,125 sq. feet and also has a two-story stack room for bound volumes of periodicals. The library provides open access to readers to the stocks while rare books section; manuscripts and archival sections and text books section observe closed access.

The library has fully computerized its most actively used collection, which is searched through OPAC. The book collection of the library is bar-coded and most active important in-house

functions like acquisition, cataloguing, circulation are automated using the virtual automation software. Also the library has license for online access for some important databases. The University library is in the process of providing its resources to the users outside the library through campus-wide Local area Network (LAN). The library has also been functioning as a referral center on Islamic Studies, Muslim, Urdu language and literature, receives requests for bibliographies on bibliographic information from all over the Country.

Collections

Library has a collection of about 3.00 lakhs books and bound volumes of periodicals, about 3000 manuscripts, 200 microfilms and subscribes to 440 journals. Library has reserved some of its collection as Textbooks collection, which is to consulted in the library or can be issued for overnight. The library is in possession of a very valuable source material on the history of freedom movement in the form of private papers of the eminent leaders such as Maulana Mohd. Ali Jauhar, Hakim Ajmal and a lot of book collections received from the eminent donors. These collections are 17 in number and are kept separately as "Special Collections.

Another Constructive feature is Jamia Authors collection which houses several hundred books written, edited and compiled by person who are or were associated with Jamia Millia Islamia.

The library is also in possession of same valuable books in the Urdu language on Vedas, Upanishads, Ramayan, Mahabharat, Bhagavat Gita, Manuscripts, Bhagwan Mahavir Gautam Budh, Guru Nanak and Sick religion, Swami Dayanand Saraswati, Swami Vivekanand, Sri Aurobindo, Radha Swami Movement etc.

Reference Collection

The Library maintains a separate reference collection consisting of fast finding tools such as almanacs, atlases, biographical and language dictionaries, directories, handbooks,

and statistical compilations. encyclopedias, technical data, almanacs, atlases, bibliographies, maps, films, books written by and on Chancellors of Jamia and Jamia Author's collection, theses and dissertations etc. These reference books are not issued as a general policy and they need to be consulted in the library. The library provides the reprographic services in this section also. . The section-in charge is equipped with providing or guiding the users to the required information. They also provide assistance in locating the misplaced books, if reported by the users

The library has fully computerized its most actively used collection, which is searched through Online Public Access Catalogue (OPAC). The OPAC allows search by author, title, subject, call number, keywords, and Boolean search etc. The call number indicates the location of the book on the self. The computer catalogue, OPAC is extremely user-friendly and enables searches to be conducted with ease and speed.

Library Collections at a Glance As on 1st May , 2003

Books	3,02,000
Journals	445
Theses	600
Microfilm/Microfiche	200
Compact Discs	30
Manuscripts	3000
Special Collections	17

Language-wise break-up of library collection is

Language	No. of books/documents
Urdu	25000
Hindi	12000
Persian	2600
Arabic	3000

10

THE LIBRARY OF TIBETAN WORKS AND ARCHIVES, DHARAMSHALA

Library of Tibetan Works and Archives (TWA) is an autonomous body under direct supervision of H.H. the Dalai Lama registered with the Government of India under the Registration of Societies Act of 1860 recognised by Himachal Pradesh University as a Centre for Research in 1991 accorded status of National Library, Achieves and Museum by Tibetan Parliament in Exile in 1996

LTWA has a governing body of nine members, three of whom represent the Government of India. The remaining six are appointed by His Holiness the Dalai Lama. This board directs policy development, oversees all major projects and departments, and provides advice and guidance for future Library initiatives. The Library's eight departments operate under the direction of the governing body.

The Library receives part of its funding from the Department of Culture and Ministry of Human Resources of the Government of India. The Library generates some of its own funding through the sale of books and publications, accommodation rental and class fees, and this is used to meet the 'major part of its budgetary needs. Public and private foundations and other philanthropic organisations such as the Ford Foundation, OXFAM India, the Smithsonian Institution, C.A.R.F., Swedish Development Co-operative, J.D.R. 3rd Fund and Uli Franz Trust, Netherlands Embassy, have provided substantial funding for specific projects in the past.

Conceived of and founded by His Holiness the 14th Dalai

Lama of Tibet, the Library of Tibetan Works and Archives (LTWA) is one of the most important institutions in the world dedicated to the preservation and dissemination of Tibetan culture. The foundation stone for the Library's Tibetan style building was laid on 11th June 1970, in the hill station of Dharamsala, north India. Located within the compound of the Tibetan Government-in-Exile, the Library serves as a repository for Tibetan artefacts and manuscripts and a centre for language and cultural education. Its holdings include more than 80,000 manuscripts, books and documents, hundreds of thangkas, statues and other artefacts, 6,000 photographs, and other materials.

As a centre for the study of Tibetan culture, the Library of Tibetan Works and Archives is firmly dedicated to a threefold vision of preservation, protection and promotion. The Library looks forward into the next century, confident of its role to preserve, and educate others about, a culture threatened with destruction. More than 25 years after its founding, the need for such an institution as the Library of Tibetan Works and Archives has continued to grow.

The primary objective of the Library of Tibetan Works and Archives is to provide a comprehensive cultural resource centre and to promote an environment fostering research and an exchange of knowledge between scholars and students. This is of the utmost importance in a contemporary world shaped by political and spiritual confusion. In trying to fulfil its objectives the Library's priorities include:

* Acquiring and conserving Tibetan books and manuscripts, artefacts and works of art;
* Providing access to books, manuscripts and reference works (in Tibetan and foreign languages) in study areas within the Library;
* Compiling bibliographies and documen-tation of library holdings and related literature available worldwide;
* Providing copies and prints of library holdings, and acting

as a reference centre for such source materials

* Publishing books and manuscripts under the Library imprint;
* Supporting research and study of the Tibetan language, classical and modern, and the traditional arts and crafts.

The Tibetan Library has been in operation since Ist November 1971. It has opened its doors to numerous scholars from many countries. It has launched educational programmes in language, philosophy, culture and the traditional arts. It has encouraged computer projects, and other initiatives aiming to preserve Tibetan thought and culture. The Library sponsors international seminars. It engages in book exchange programmes with other libraries and distributes its own publications, in Tibetan and English, throughout the world. Library holdings increase every year and class enrollments in the

Centre for Tibetan Studies continue to climb. The Library is home to one of only two Tibetan Oral History projects in the world. Its dynamic thangka painting and woodcarving programmes are indica-tive of the fact that cultural preservation includes the arts as well as letters. LTWA works in close collaboration with the Central Institute for Higher Tibetan Studies (deemed a university) in Sarnath and the Department of Religion and Culture of the Central Tibetan Administration. With each year of operation increasing numbers of visitors, researchers and students are drawn to this institution which is able to provide them with an educational and cultural experience available nowhere else in the world.

Departments of the LTWA

The Library is organized in eight distinct departments:

1. The Library itself, which consists of the Tibetan Manuscript Collection and The Foreign Language Reference Library.
2. The Archives, consisting of the Document and Photographic Archives.

3. The Museum.
4. Education, operating the Centre for Tibetan Studies, which administers courses in Philosophy and Tibetan Language.
5. Research and Translation.
6. Publications.
7. Oral History.
8. Administration.

The Libraries

The Library holds 70,000 manuscripts and documents in Tibetan and 10,000 books in English and foreign languages dealing with Buddhism and Tibet related affairs.

Between them, the Tibetan Manuscript Collection and the Foreign Language Reference Library contain more than 80,000 items, ranging from handwritten manuscripts and centuries old documents to contemporary books and periodicals. Parts of the collection are open to the public, while access to others is restricted to accredited scholars and researchers. Study areas are provided in the respective wings housing each collection. Research guidance is available from many resident scholars at the Library. General information about the libraries is available at the reception desk on the ground floor.

The Tibetan Manuscript Collection maintains holdings of more than 70,000 manuscripts, xylographs, documents, illuminated manuscripts and microfilm records. This is the most important collection of such materials in the world. Of special value are several handwritten editions of the Kangyur and Tengyur, the Tibetan Buddhist Canon; sixteen handwritten volumes of sundry collected works from Phudrag Monastery and sixteen additional volumes commissioned by Tsagta, Chief of Eastern Kongpo in the 15th century. The major works of Tibet's four Buddhist traditions, the Nyingma, Kagyu, Sakya and Gelug, as well as the indigenous Bön tradition, constitute the main body of the collection.

The Library maintains manuscript exchange projects with many institutions around the world. These include the Gorky Scientific Library in Leningrad; the Ulan Bator State Library in Mongolia; the Sikkim Research Institute in Gangtok; the National Library of the Royal Government of Bhutan; Toyo-Bunko in Japan, and the Beijing National Library. In special cases these institutions provide and exchange photocopies of rare and important works which are otherwise unavailable for general circulation or loan.

The Tibetan Manuscript Collection acquires new materials from among those donated to His Holiness the Dalai Lama as well as from direct acquisitions in Tibet. Several hundred volumes are added each year, ranging from rare and original manuscripts to contemporary reprints in book form. The Tibetan Manuscript Collection is in the process of completing a general catalogue of all materials in the collection. This task is made more difficult by the nature of the holdings and the tendency for works to have elaborate titles containing similar epithets and for authors to be known by a variety of names. The entire collection is also being catalogued in a computer database in the Tibetan language, which will be available to the public. This makes it the only collection of its kind catalogued by computer in Tibetan.

The Foreign Language Reference Library has a collection of more than 10,000 volumes predominantly dealing with language, philosophy, arts and culture, medicine, geography, travel, history and politics of Tibet and the Himalayan region. These materials are primarily in English, but include some in major European and Indian languages, as well as Japanese, Chinese, Russian, and Mongolian. More than 120 journals and periodicals of related interest are currently received and displayed. There is a modest collection of rare and out-of-print books, files of newspaper clippings covering the past 25 years of the Tibetan diaspora, bound collections of periodicals, and files of pamphlets, brochures and other materials concerning the Tibetan community dating back to 1959. Holdings can be

accessed through an online cataloguing system. Books are kept in a separate stack room, from where librarians retrieve them on request. The reading room is divided between an area of large open tables and a set of individual study booths.

The continuing expansion of the Foreign Language collection is matched by its growing number of patrons. New acquisitions are received each year from various sources in addition to outright purchases. Publication exchange programmes provide volumes from other publishers and libraries in exchange for new books brought out by the LTWA's Publication Department. Copies of doctoral dissertations are regularly received from University Microfilm International. Books are also donated each year by visiting scholars and by other institutions not formally part of the publication exchange programme. On average, 2,000 people enrol as members of the Library each year for a small fee. They are entitled to use the resources within the reference room. Only accredited research scholars are allowed to borrow materials. Limited photocopying can be done by request on the Library premises.

The Archives

Several thousand legal and social documents in Tibetan, some dating back as far as the 10th century and 6,000 photographs, negatives and slides of Tibet.

The Document and Photographic Archives have seen rapid growth in recent years. Documents include government edicts and court proclamations, marriage and land contracts and others, which reveal otherwise unrecorded aspects of Tibetan life. Many scholars consult these, and the Photographic Archives' collection of negatives and slides, which includes black and white and colour photographs taken by American travellers Tolstoy and Dolan in the 1940s. Many photographs are displayed in the Library itself.

An important new project for the LTWA is the launch of the Central Archives of the Works of His Holiness the 14th Dalai Lama. The purpose of this Archive, as its name implies, is to

gather together all materials concerning His Holiness the Dalai Lama's teachings, writings and speeches. Contri-butions have been received from all over the world.

The Library is also host to a newly initiated Architectural Archive which consists of a catalogued collection of photographs of buildings and architectural features in Tibet and the Himalayan region. Many of the buildings recorded in this Archive no longer exist. Consequently, the collection provides an invaluable glimpse of Tibet's erstwhile magnificent architectural heritage. A Tibetan Architectural Club has been established in this connection to encourage local Tibetan school students with an interest in architecture to develop an appreciation of Tibetan building traditions.

The Museum

There are 600 statues and thangka paintings and several hundred reliquary and other ritual objects, some dating back to the 12th century three-dimensional carved wood mandala of Avalokiteshvara

The Museum, located on the first floor of the Library, originated as a repository of art and artefacts offered to His Holiness the Dalai Lama. It was laid out in consultation with the National Museum of India and opened to the public in 1974. The Museum has expanded steadily since those early days and now exhibits one of the most important collections of Tibetan art in the world. Major exhibits include a three-dimensional carved wooden mandala of Avalokiteshvara and a thread-cross mandala of Arya Tara, both commissioned by the LTWA; a bronze statue of Avalokiteshvara commissioned by the 13th Dalai Lama, said to stand as tall as he did; and a contemporary life-size statue of Je Tsongkhapa.

The Museum commissions works by local artists, loans objects to international institutions for exhibition, and trains library employees in preservation techniques.

The Education Department

Department of education has a provision for courses in Buddhist philosophy taught by highly qualified masters courses in classical and colloquial Tibetan language, thangka painting and woodcarving schools

The Centre for Tibetan Studies is administered by the Education Department and is recognised by the Himachal Pradesh University in Shimla. It offers courses for the growing number of people interested in Tibetan language, philosophy and art. Classes were first taught in 1971 and have grown steadily in scope and attendance ever since. The Centre's work is an important aspect of the Library's effort to both sustain and extend appreciation and understanding of Tibetan culture.

Classes in Tibetan language and philosophy meet six days a week. Two different courses run concurrently in each of the programmes. Language classes run three terms of three months each, while the duration of the philosophy courses depends on the texts that are being studied. The academic year is 10 months long, from March to December each year. A class schedule is published annually by the Education Department. Full term intensive courses in Tibetan language and literary appreciation are conducted for members of the Central Tibetan Administration and allied institutions every year.

Philosophy classes are taught by Geshes selected by the LTWA Board for their experience and good reputation. Their explanations are usually given in Tibetan and are translated into English by experienced interpreters. Classic Tibetan and Indian Buddhist texts are selected as the focus of study to provide a first-hand knowledge of Buddhist philosophy, meditation, psychology and ethics. The student body typically includes Tibetan and foreign students and postgraduate scholars. Classes include meditation practice, lectures and discussion of texts and scriptures. These courses are popular, an average of 100 students attending each.

Language classes are taught by teachers fluent in both Tibetan and English. They cover spoken and written Tibetan, aspects of grammar and idiomatic speech, and are intended to equip students to study Tibetan culture and religion. Colloquial and classical Tibetan are dealt with in advanced classes. Many of the texts used in classes have been published by the LTWA. Class sizes average 30 students. Students from more than 20 countries have registered for these courses.

The Education Department also operates schools of thangka painting and traditional woodcarving. Established in 1977 and 1982 respectively, both schools conduct intensive five-year apprenticeship programmes. Almost 50 artists, who continue the traditional Tibetan arts in India and elsewhere, have trained in this school. These courses are taught by renowned master artists.

Thangka painting is one of the most important aspects of traditional Tibetan culture. It is regarded as a reflection of the life and imagination of the Tibetan mind. The education of a thangka painter goes far beyond mere painting techniques. Iconography, Tibetan philosophy, and art history are all aspects of the training.

Traditional Tibetan woodcarving has been given a new lease of life by the master artists of the school. Students construct altars, shrines, three-dimensional mandalas, and other objects for use in temples and monasteries.

Research and translation department

The Library provides expert research assistance for 50-60 foreign scholars per year translation of Tibetan literature for publication

This department provides vital services to the Publication and Education Departments of the Library. It supports scholarly research in all fields of Tibetan thought.

The translation department is staffed by Tibetan scholars who are assisted in their work by native English speakers. The

team translates texts for the Publication Department and compiles translations of the daily Buddhist philosophy classes. LTWA translators also provide services for other branches of the Tibetan Government-in-Exile in Dharamsala.

Recognising the lack of skilled translators fluent in both Tibetan and English, LTWA held a seminar at the Central Institute for Higher Tibetan Studies at Sarnath, Varanasi in 1991, to assess the Tibetan community's future translation needs. As a result of this seminar, training courses have subsequently been held.

The research section assists the growing number of scholars who visit the LTWA and corresponds with other institutions around the world. The Department's highly qualified staff includes scholars who have graduated in traditional Tibetan monasteries and others who have trained in contemporary universities.

The Department welcomes an average of 50-60 foreign scholars per year. Staff have access to microfilm and microfiche readers, and computer facilities for word processing and cataloguing in the Tibetan language.

Publication

The publications of the Library include two periodicals, Tibet Journal and Tibetan Medicine, 300 publications to date in English concerning Buddhist philosophy and other aspects of Tibetan culture and 140 publication to date in Tibetan

The Publications Department publishes and distributes a wide range of publications concerning Tibetan studies worldwide. The department produces numerous publications annually in both Tibetan and English, in close co-operation with the Translation and Research Departments.

Two periodicals, Tibet Journal and Tibetan Medicine, are regarded with high esteem in Tibetan academic circles throughout the world. The Tibet Journal, a scholarly quarterly in English, first appeared in 1975. It features articles on Tibetan history, art, philosophy, literature and language, and includes book reviews.

Some special editions have been dedicated to single topics such as the Tibetan Government and court systems, the Muslim community and the visual arts. The journal also publishes articles related to Nepal, Bhutan, Mongolia and the Trans-himalayan regions which have geographical and cultural affinities to Tibet.

Tibetan Medicine, an annual publication, first appeared in 1980. It features articles on specific aspects of Tibetan medicine, extensive interviews with Tibetan doctors and medical practitioners, and information on medical history and medicinal plants. It is one of the few periodicals in the world solely dedicated to research, study and the dissemination of traditional Tibetan medicine.

The English section predominantly publishes texts concerned with Buddhist philosophy, but has also brought out books relating to Tibetan archeology, history, politics, medicine, language, folk culture and proverbs. Native English speakers functioning as editors work in a team with Tibetan translators. Titles published to date range from the classic Guide to the Bodhisattva 's Way of Life by translators. Titles published to date range from the classic Guide to the Bodhisattva's Way of Life by Shantideva, to the current Cultivating a Daily Meditation by His Holiness the Dalai Lama. The publications are distributed worldwide by the Delhi-based Paljor Publications, a branch of the Charitable Trust of H.H. The Dalai Lama.

The Tibetan section publishes an average of six books a year, and has brought out more than 142 titles since 1972. While the sale of publications provides operating funds for the Library in general, their wide distribution serves to raise global awareness of Tibetan culture.

Oral History Department

The Library has one of only two such projects in the work 15,000 hours of taped interviews with senior Tibetans, recording both religious and secular life in audio and video formats

The Oral History Project was begun in 1976. Since then

taped interviews with elders, Lamas and other religious figures, crafts people, doctors and astrologers, story-tellers, traders and pilgrims have been recorded. Oral traditions are very susceptible to permanent loss should their transmission be interrupted. Some of the oral records archived are unique, traditionally passed only from one person to another. Nevertheless, they have been recorded to preserve them for the future.

This project is unique in documenting important aspects of folk culture in India and Tibet in the Tibetan language. The Department has transcribed some of its recordings, but as potential interviewees grow older and more fragile, priority has been given to recording their reminiscences. Most recordings are conducted by retired government employees and volunteers within the Tibetan refugee community.

The Oral History Archives contain hundreds of hours of teachings by His Holiness the Dalai Lama; accounts of the journey from Tibet to India; Tibetan proverbs and stories; explanations of Tibetan healing methods; and descriptions of traditional dress, costumes and ornaments, songs and dances. The Department has embarked on developing a computerised catalogue of its recordings, as well as the production of printed transcripts and English translations of selected interviews.

11

THE NATIONAL LIBRARY OF INDIA, KOLKATTA

The National Library of India has a long history. It came into existence in 1948 after passing through various stages of development. The National Library of India is located in Kolkata (Calcutta). It is the largest library in the country. It is an institution of national importance under the Department of Culture, Ministry of Tourism and Culture, Government of India. With the passing of Imperial Library (Change of Name) Act 1948. In the same year, it was shifted to Belvedere Estate, its present location, which was the former viceregal palace. It is now housed in three separate buildings with a separate preservation laboratory. It was formally opened to the public on 1st February 1953 by the late Maulana Abul Kalam Azad, the then Union Education Minister. The origin of the library, however, can be traced dating back to March 1836, when the Calcutta Public Library was opened to the public at 30 Esplanade Row, Calcutta. Subsequently the Calcutta Public Library was merged with the Imperial Library in January 1903.

The Library's responsibility is to collect, disseminate and preserve the printed heritage of the country. It's also one of the oldest institutions of the country focussed on the conservation and maintenance of the bibliographic documents in various fields of knowledge. The National Library of India is celebrating its centenary year with some new initiatives and challenges. Digitization of manuscripts is one such initiative the library has taken up responding to the growing use and adaptability of information technology to library-related activities.

The first name of the National Library was Calcutta Public

Library which was established in 1836. It was not a Government institution. It was running on a proprietary basis. Every person subscribing Rs. 300/- in one payment or three instalments was to be considered a proprietor. Poor students and others were allowed to use the library free of charge for a specified period of time. The then Governor General, Lord Metcalf transferred 4,675 volumes from the library of the College of Fort William to the Calcutta Public Library. This and donations of books from individuals formed the nucleus of the library. Prince Dwarkanath Tagore was the first proprietor of the Calcutta Public Library.

Both the Indian and foreign books, specially from Britain, were purchased for the library. In the report of 1850 we find that the library started collecting books in Gujarati, Marathi, Pali, Ceylonese and Punjabi. Donations were regularly made by individuals as well as by the Government of Bengal and North Western Provinces.

The Calcutta Public Library had a unique position as the first public library in this part of the country. Such a well-organised and efficiently run library was rare even in Europe during the first half of the 19th century. Because of the efforts of the Calcutta Public Library, the National Library has many extremely rare books and journals in its collection.

The Imperial Library

The Imperial Library was formed in 1891 by combining a number of Secretariat libraries. Of these, the most important and interesting was the library of the Home Department, which contained many books formerly belonging to the library of East India College, Fort William and the library of the East India Board in London. But the use of the library was restricted to the superior officers of the Government.

Amalgamation of CPL and Imperial Library

Lord Curzon, the then Governor General of India, was the person who conceived the idea of opening a library for the use of the public. He noticed both the libraries — Imperial Library and

Calcutta Public Library — were under-utilised for the want of facilities or restrictions. So, he decided to amalgamate the rich collection of both of these libraries. He was successful in effecting the amalgamation of Calcutta Public Library with the then Imperial Library under certain terms.

John Macfarlane, the Asst. Librarian of the British Museum, London, was appointed as the first Librarian of the Imperial Library. After his death, the famous scholar and linguist Harinath De took over the charge of the library. After his death J. A. Chapman became the librarian. Mr. Chapman showed keen interest in the affairs of the library and tried hard to improve its status. After his retirement, Khan Bahadur M.A. Asadulla was appointed as the librarian and he continued as the librarian till July 1947.

The policy of acquisition broadly adhered to by the Imperial Library was enunciated by Lord Curzon in his speech at the opening ceremony of the library, — "The general idea of the whole Library is that it should contain all the books that have been written about India in popular tongues, with such additions as are required to make it a good all-round library of standard works of reference.

Declaring the Imperial Library as the National Library

After the independence the Government of India changed the name of the Imperial Library as the National Library, with an enactment of the Imperial Library (change of name) Act 1948. and the collection was shifted from the Esplanade to the present Belvedere Estate. On 1st February 1953 the National Library was opened to the public, inaugurated by Maulana Abul Kalam Azad. Sri B.S. Kesavan was appointed as the first librarian of the National Library.

English Language Collection

The National Library has an invaluable collection in English language, because of the systematic collection development by Calcutta Public Library as well as by the Imperial

Library. Way back in 1848 itself, an attempt was being made to acquire journals issued by the foreign learned institutions. Serious works were purchased in large numbers than the light literature. Now a days also the same policy is being continued.

At present the library has a rich collection of English books and other reading materials in almost all the subjects. The collection is extremely rich in humanities, British and Indian history and literature.

Foreign languages collections

One of the aims of the National Library is to collect all the books published on India, anywhere in the world and in any language. At the same time it is also collecting a fair collection of reading materials in different languages for the use of the country.

Imperial library had a good number of Arabic and Persian works and few other foreign language books. In 1985 European Languages Division was reorganized and five separate divisions were formed. They are: East Asian Languages Division, Germanic Languages Division, Romance Languages Division, Slavonic Languages Division, West Asian and African Languages Division .

The foreign language works are mainly acquired through purchase, Gift and exchange. All the above language divisions are responsible for collection development, collection organisation and information dissemination to the readers in their respective languages. They also maintain their own stacks and provide reading facilities to the readers.

East Asian Languages Collection

A separate division was established to collect, process and preserve Chinese and other East Asian languages. At present the collection has 15,000 Chinese and one thousands each in Japanese, Korean, Tibetan, Nepali and Thai languages.

first printer, publisher and writer of Calcutta, are very well represented in this collection. The following rare books published by Lulloo Lal are in the library: Braja Bhasha Grammar (1811), Lataife Hindi (1821) and Rajaniti (1827). Prem Sagur (1842).

Apart from the above publications, the library has — The oriental linguist with an Extensive vocabulary English and Hindoostanee and Hindoostanee and English by John B. Gilchrist (1798), Hindi-Roman Orthoepigraphical Ultimatum... by John B. Gilchrist (1804), Rajneeti by Narayana Pandit (1809), Sudamacaritra by Haldhara Dasa(1819), Raga Kalpadruma (1843), Baital Pachisi by Duncan Forbes (1861), Dictionary of Hindee and English by J. T. Thompson (1862), Yavan Bhasa Ka Vyakaran by Hooper William (1874), Siva Simha Saroja by Siva Simha Senagar (1878), Hindi Pradipa edited by Balkrishna Bhatt (1877-1909), Brief account of the Solar system in Hindi (1940), and a microfilm copy of 'Bal Bodhini,' (1874 - 1877)— a monthly Journal for women edited by Bharatendu Harischandra. There are also about 1200 rare first issues of important journals in this collection.

The division also has a good number of Maithili books.

Kannada Language Collection

A separate Kannada division came into existence in 1963 in the National Library, to collect and preserve the books and other published materials in Kannada language. In 1960, the library purchased the personal collection of H. Channakeshava Ayyangar. This collection consists of 1300 books published between the last two decades of the 19th century and the first three decades of the 20th century. The efforts of G.P. Rajaratnam, a noted Kannada author, in building the Kannada collection in the library is worth mentioning. Immediately after the enactment of the D.B. Act, Rajaratnam toured erstwhile Mysore state to create awareness among the publishers about the Act. He also collected about 1,500 books on behalf of the library and sent them to the library, with out any expense to the library. The

Kannada collection in the library is very useful for the study of cultural history of Karnataka.

At present there are 32,000 Kannada books in the library.

Kashmiri Language Collection

Kashmiri division became an independent division in 1983. Now the library has 500 Kashmir books. Some of the important publications available in this collection are : Muhammad Yusuf Teng's Shirin Qalm (2 Volumes), Wiyur edited by Ghulam Muhammad Rafiq, Ghulam Nabi Khyal's Akah Nandun, Nurnama (Sayings of Nuruddin Wali) and compiled by Muhammad Amin Kaim, Fazil and Kashmiri's Krishna Lila.

Malayalam Language Collection

Malayalam division, as a separate division, was established in the National Library in 1963. Then the division had 5,000 books. Now the collection has 34,500 books. The earliest printed book available in the collection dates back to 1791, Centum Adagia Malabarica is a Latin translation of Malayalam proverbs. Both the Malayalam originals and Latin translations are printed side by side. Among the many rare and old books, mention may be made of the following works: Robert Drummond's Grammar of the Malabar Language (1799), Dr. Gundart's Malayalam—English dictionary (1872) Vartamanapustakam by Parammachkal Govarnnodoracchan, Appu Nedungadi's Kundalata and Chantu Menan's. Indulekha (1889). Apart from these, many works representing the early periods are also available in this collection. Few of them are: Ramacaritam, (earliest known Malayalam work), works of Niranam (15th Century poet), Cerussery's Krishnagatha (16th century), Vatakkan Pattukal (Ballads of North Malabar), Ezuttachan's Adhyatama Ramayana, Ramaprattu Variyar's Kucelavrtam, Kuncan Nampyar's Tullol.

Marathi Language Collection

Marathi division was established in 1963 with a collection of 8900 volumes, to collect and process Marathi books in the

National Library. Now the division has 37,000 books in its collection. In 1954 the National Library purchased the library of the Bengal Nagpur Railway Indian Institure, Kharagpur which had a good number of Marathi books. Sir Jadunath Sarkar Collection also has about 350 Marathi books, on the history of Maratha period. The division has many rare and old Marathi Publications. Few of them are: William Carey's — A grammar of the Mahratta language (1805) and Dictionary of the Maharatta language (1810), Simhasana battisi (1814), Raghuji Bhinsalyanihi vanshavali (1815), Vans Kennedy's — A dictionary of Maratta language (1824), Nava Karar (1850), A Short Account of Railways by K. Bhatwadekar (1854), Charles Hutton's Bijaganit (1856), Vishnu Parashuram Pandit and Shankar Pandurang Pandit edited Tukaram's Abhangachi gatha (1869), H. A. Acworth edited Itihasaprisiddha purushanche va striyanche povade (1891).

Oriya Language Collection

A separate Oriya division was established in 1973, in the National Library, to acquire and process Oriya books. Imperial Library had only 133 books, later the collection was increased to 425 books. Now the division has 19500 books.

The oldest publication available in the Oriya collection dates back to 1831. It is Rev. Amos Sutton's Introductory Grammar of Oriya language . Some of the other rarities in the collection are: Jayadeva's Gitagovinda, translated by Dharanidhara, Amos Sutton's An Oriya dictionary — 3 vols.(1841-1843), Dharmapustakara Adibhaya (1842-1843). Purnacandra Odiabhasa Kosh (1931-1940), a lexicon of Oriya language compiled by Gopalachandra Praharaj.

Punjabi Language Collection

A separate division for the acquisition and processing of Punjabi language books, was established in 1974. Most of the works in this collection are of recent origin. But still the collection has few old and rare Punjabi books. Some of them are : William Carey's A Grammar of Punjabee Language (1812). Samuel

Starkey's A Dictionary of English Punjabee (1849), Geographical Description of the Panjab (1850), Bhai Santosh Singh's Guru Paratap Suraj Granthavali (1882) and Gurudas Bhai's Vars (1893).

Sanskrit, Pali and Prakrit languages Collection

Sanskrit has the rich heritage of literature in all the spheres of knowledge. A separate division is functioning in the National Library to collect and process Sanskrit books. At present the division has over 20,000 Sanskrit books, printed in Devnagari script. Almost all Indian Language divisions possess Sanskrit works printed in their respective language scripts. The Library also has a rich collection of Sanskrit works edited or translated with original scripts, in English and many other foreign language.

The collection is so rich, that it attracts scholars both from India and abroad. Apart from Sanskrit, books in Pail and Prakrit languages are also collected and processed by this division. At present the library has about 500 books in Pali and a similar number of books in Prakrit

Sindhi Language Collection

Since 1957, Sindhi books are being added in the National Library. At present the Library has 2,100 Sindhi books. Shah Abdul Latif's Shah Jo Rasalo and Shah Jo Sher are the prized works in this collection

Tamil Language Collection

Tamil division was formed in 1963 in the library. At present the division has 57,000 books. Apart from this, the Library has 1000 Tamil books and 300 Tamil Manuscripts in Vaipuri Pillai collection. The library has many rare and old Tamil works. Earliest printed Tamil books available in the library are: Tamil Bible (1723); John Philip Fabricius's A Malabar and English Dictionary (1779); Tamil translation of John Bunyan's Piligrim's progress (1793); Caldwell's Comparative Grammar of Dravidian languages (1850). The collection also includes standard editions of five great Sangam Classics.

Telugu Language Collection

Telugu division was formed in the National Library in 1963. The collection has good number of old Telugu books published since the earlier decades of the 19th Century. Some of the Telugu language rarities available in this collection are: William Carey's Grammar of Telugu language (1814); C. P. Brown's A vocabulary of Gentoo and English (1818); Vakyavali (1852); Catalogue of Telugu books in the British library, London, (1912) compiled by L. D. Barnett

Urdu Language Collection

Like Arabic and Persian collection, Urdu language collection was also well developed from the days of Imperial library. Buhar library, Hidayat Husain collection, Zakariya Collection. Imambara collection also have some Urdu books and manuscripts. In 1968 a separate Urdu division was formed in the Library. At present the collection has more than 20,000 books. Some of the oldest books in this collection are: Uklakhi Hindee or Indian Ethics (1803), Mir Muhamad Takis Kulliuat- e- Mir (1811).

Rare Books

The National Library has innumerable number of rare books and other reading materials. Earlier, these items were stacked with other books. But, in 1973, a separate Rare Books Division was established to take care of the rare books. At present the books published prior to 1860 are considered as rare books. Along with such materials, manuscripts and microfilms of the library are also stacked in this division. The division also provides reading facilities to the users who wish to consult these items. At present the division has 4,700 monographs, 3000 manuscripts and 1500 microfilms.

Science and Technology Collection

As per the recommendations of the 'Reviewing Committee' (1968), Science and Technology Division was set up in 1972. in

the National Library, India. The basic function of this division is to collect and disseminate the core material in science and technology. At present the division holds about 17,000 books and monographs and 800 titles of current periodicals. The division provides reading facilities to the users. This is the only division which has an open access stack system.

Indian Official Documents

All the publications of Government of India, State Governments, Union Territories, Government Undertakings, Autonomous Bodies are collected, processed and preserved separately. A separate division for this purpose was established in 1972. The Library owns a very rich collection of Indian official documents from the days of East India Company to the present day. The collection also includes the documents published by the Government of Great Britain relating to India. A good collection of Burmese documents and few documents of Aden, Ceylon, Persian Gulf Political Residency are also part of this collection. At present the division has 4, 90,000 documents.

Foreign Official Documents

The National Library is one of the repository libraries for United Nations organisation and its agencies. Thus all the publications of U.N.O. and its agencies are received by the library free of cost. These documents are processed and stacked separately. The library also receives publications of the Governments of United States of America, Great Britain, Canada, Commonwealth Nations, and the publications of European Economic Committee. Almost all the volumes of the sessional sets of British Parliamentary papers since the beginning of the 19th century are also available.

Apart from the depositary copies, the Library also acquires selected foreign publications through purchase. At present the Library has 400,000 foreign official documents.

All the newspapers and periodicals of Indian languages are received and processed in their respective language divisions.

But English newspapers and periodicals - both the Indian and foreign, are acquired and processed separately. Separate Serials division is responsible for acquiring and processing of English Newspapers and periodicals. Library has a rich collection of late 19th and early 20th century newspapers and periodicals, but almost all of them are incomplete. The catalogue of periodicals, newspapers and gazettes available in the library up to 1953 is available

West Asian and African Languages Collection

Buhar Library may be considered as the nucleus of West Asian and African languages collection. Though this division has a handful of books in other West Asian languages, like Hebrew and Amharic. The largest number of books is in Persian and Arabic languages. Approximately 12,000 Arabic and 12,000 Persian language books are in the collection. The collection includes the lexicons compiled and prepared by Indians authors of the past and edited by the 'native' scholars of the college of Fort William and European orientalists of the said college. The division also holds a large numbers of historical works published under the 'Bibliotheca Indica' of the Asiatic Society of Bengal in the 19th century.

Large number of Arabic and Persian books and manuscripts can also be seen in Sir Abdur Rahim Collection, Hidayat Husain Collection, Zakaria Collection and Imambara Collection. Even Jadunath Sarkar collection also has 200 Persian manuscripts. This collection of manuscripts is especially rich in works on the later Mughal Period (1659-1837) and the early British regime of India.

Manuscripts

National Library has about 3600 rare and historically important manuscripts in different languages. These manuscripts are preserved separately along with other important and rare books in the Rare Books Division. The xylographs presented by H.E. the Dalai Lama are also preserved in this collection.

In a way it is an extension of the earlier project, the content

being the only difference. The National Library has in its possession a small holding of manuscripts representing some basic and important branches of knowledge. These manuscript collections are mostly part of some collections belonging to eminent personalities of India, which were donated by their heirs. The details of the holdings are as follows:

1. Paper Manuscripts: 3000 volumes approximately.
2. Correspondence and diaries: 250 volumes approximately.
3. Palm Leaf Manuscripts: 334 volumes approximately

The following is the language-wise break-up of the manuscripts:

a. Arabic: 681
b. Persian: 955
c. Urdu: 21
d. Bengali: 162
e. English: 255
f. Hindi: 5
g. Tamil: 370
h. Sanskrit:790

While the Tamil manuscripts in palm leaves are unique in character, the Arabic and Persian manuscripts bear beautiful illustrations, fine calligraphy and elegant bindings. Loose letters, diaries.

Maps and Prints

The library has a rich collection of maps. The collection ranges from 17th century onwards. Indian topographical sheets of earlier days (at scale of one inch, half inch and quarter inch to a mile) and maps of natural resources, population, transport and communication systems, agricultural production, Soil, Vegetation and Geology of India form the major part of the collection. At present the library has 85,000 printed maps, 54 cartographic manuscripts and 280 atlases.

Microforms

The Library has 500 rolls of Microfilms and 1000 Microfiches. These are preserved in the Rare Books division. Census of India (1872-1951) is one of the most important and rare document available in the form of Microfiches.

12
OSMANIA UNIVERSITY LIBRARY, HYDERABAD

Osmania University, established in 1918, is the seventh oldest in India, the third oldest in south India and the first to be established in the erstwhile princely state of Hyderabad. Throughout its existence of over eight decades, it has shown remarkable progress and sustained an integrated development of all faculties. It has significantly contributed to the academic and economic development of not only the region but also of the Country. Its alumni have distinguished themselves nationally and internationally in various spheres of life and are spread far and wide around the world.

With a sprawling campus of nearly 1600 acres and buildings of majestic beauty and architectural splendor, Osmania University, is perhaps, the largest higher education system in the Country. It is a home to nearly 300,000 students pursuing their higher studies in its Campus, Constituent, Affiliated Colleges and District Centres. Its faculty and staff number nearly 5000. It is a multi-faculty and multidisciplinary university, offering rich and varied courses in the fields of Humanities, Arts, Sciences, Social Sciences, Law, Engineering, Technology, Commerce and Business Management, Information Technology and Oriental Languages. The University's strategic planning, teaching-and-learning policies and research direction have always emphasized respect for the concerns of the society and the need to address the issues that challenge it.

In recognition of its excellent academic achievements, Osmania University had the distinction of being awarded the

FIVE STAR status by the National Accreditation and Assessment Council (NAAC) of the University Grants Commission, Government of India in the year 2001.

One of the prime endeavors of the University has been to bring-in required changes in course contents along with innovations in the delivery of Higher Education. Consequently appropriate design and introduction of new courses, that are so essential for an active engagement with the community around, have always been its hallmark.

To be the premier institution that offers teaching and learning programmes of the best quality, graduate students who excel and become leaders in the chosen profession contributing to the community, the nation and the world, and prepares individuals of the highest moral fibre.

The mission of the University includes the following:

* To achieve excellence in teaching and research.
* To preserve and generate knowledge.
* To cultivate resolute moral values
* To develop and enhance human resources.
* To improve the quality of life and contribute to sustainable development of the region and the nation in harmony with our culture, heritage and environment

About the Library

The University library system consists of a Main Library and College / Department/Seminar Libraries. The University Library coordinates the library system which links the libraries in all the campus and constituent college libraries.

The main library was established in 1918 along with the University. The Library was shifted to the present building which was inaugurated by Dr. S. Radhakrishnan, the then President of India on 3rd August, 1963. The main library building departs from the traditional use of the Indo-Sarcenic arch, but it seeks unity with the older buildings of the campus through the dominant

pillars of the entrance portal. It stands majestically inviolable on the highest point of the campus, commanding a panoramic view of the unusually beautiful Deccan landscape. The new building has a floor area of 62,000 sq.ft. It is a fitting symbol of the present decade of progress. The Library is divided into a number of Sections basing on the collection and services offered. They are Text Book Section, Periodical Section, Reference Section, Acquisition & Cataloguing Sections. Additionally, it has Vision of Osmania, Manuscript Section, Thesis Section, CERL Section & U.N. Section, which are highlighted.

Library Collections

The main Library holds nearly 4,00,000 books and 6428 manuscripts including rare palm leaf manuscripts. It has subscribed to about 400 learned periodicals/journals in various subjects. Also subscribes a number of newspapers. Back issues of learned periodicals are bound and preserved for future reference. The library also houses a collection of compact discs received along with books and also has LISA, PSYCHILIT, Supreme Court Cases on CDs, audio-cassettes of TOFEL, etc. are available in the Computer Section of the Library for the benefit of its members.

United Nations Depository Library

Osmania University Library is a U.N. Depository since 1966. It receives about 500 documents, 250 journals and mimeographed documents annually against a token subscription of US $300. Almost all the publications of UN and its organs, agencies, committees and commissions are being received by the Library regularly. Presently, the Library has about 12,000 documents in its collection. They are classified and arranged according to organization wise. A quarterly documentation list is prepared and circulated for the use of faculty, scholars and students. The collection is very rich and useful for reference, study and research. It is meant for reference within the library premises and is not lent for home reading.

Every year the Osmania University Library celebrates the important days like International Literary Day on September 8th, Human Rights Day on 10th December and a weeklong programme on the occasion of United Nations Day from October 24-30th. These days are celebrated by holding book exhibitions, symposiums, lectures, elocution competitions, etc. The main purpose of the programme is to create the awareness about the United Nations and its agencies, to highlight their importance and their services in the pursuit of international peace and world development. The literature brought out by the U.N. systems is comprehensive and very useful for the researchers and academic community. Hence the University Library acquires and maintains the collection as a special collection and provides bibliographical and documentation services to the readers. The reading material available in the UN Depository Library comprises of Yearbooks, Reports, Handbooks, Annual Reports, Working papers, Project Reports, Proceedings, Minutes, Agenda and other notifications. Additionally, there are also journals and serials and mimeographed documents, etc., which are also very much in use by scholars.

Following are some of the UN publications available in the Depository library.

* Demographic Yearbook 1996
* Energy Statistics Yearbook 1194
* International Trade Statistics Yearbook 1996
* Statistical Yearbook for Asia & the Pacific 1997
* UNCTAD Commodity Yearbook 1992
* UN Disarmament Yearbook 1992
* Yearbook of the Human Rights Committee 1993
* Yearbook of the International Law Commission 1994
* Yearbook of the United Nations 1994
* Yearbook of Human Rights 1994
* Basic facts about the United Nations 1994

* World Bank Reports 1983
* World Economic outlook 1996
* Proceedings of the Conference on Trade and Development 1996

During the last two years, it is found that some of the regular publications are not being received or there is a considerable delay in receiving the UN Publications. It is not possible to satisfy the needs of the reader's without the latest publications.

Awareness among the students has been increased considerably. There is a demand for material on environment, economic conditions, human rights, women's studies, etc. It will be appropriate if the UN considers our requirement and send us material on these subjects in printed/electronic form. The library has Internet facility.

Manuscripts

The Library has 6428 manuscripts including palm-leaf manuscripts in Arabic, Hebrew, Hindi, Kannada, Marathi, Persian, Sanskrit, Tamil, Telugu, Turkish and Urdu languages and cover a variety of subjects. This collection is rare and valuable for study and research. A notable feature is that the Library has two Manuscripts of Mahabharata and one Manuscript of Bhagavata.

Mahabharata Manuscripts

The two manuscripts of Mahabharata are of two different sizes, one is of 18" × 6" and the other is of 20" × 10.1/4". Both of them are valuable not only with regard to the text and commentaries, but also from the artistic point of view.

The first manuscript contains almost the whole text of the Mahabharata with Nilakanta's commentary. Every page of the Manuscript has distinctive gold and silver border interspersed with floral designs. Each page contains miniature paintings of the characters mentioned in the text on that particular page. The manuscripts contains two dates one in the beginning and the other

towards the end. The former is Saka 1722 (A.D. 1800) and the latter is Saka 1751 (A.D.1829). It can be gleaned from this that it took 29 years for the manuscript to be copied and illustrated

The second manuscript does not cover the whole text, but there is one bundle of Bhishma Parva which requires special mention. It contains the Bhagavadgita with three commentaries, the text occupying the middle and the three commentaries occupying the upper and the lower portions with floral borders. There are miniature paintings of Krishna and Arjuna on each page. In addition to the above there are different battle scenes which are of great interest. Though the manuscript is more than one hundred and fifty years old the colours are still fresh. The script used is both of the Bombay and Bengal variety. There is a note in the manuscript stating that it was copied at Bhagyanagar (Hyderabad) on the banks of the Muchkunda (Musi).

Bhagavata Manuscript

This Section has an illustrated scroll of the complete text of the 12 Skandhas of Srimadbhagavata. The scroll is 4 inches wide and 64 ft.long. This is a unique manuscript of the Dasama Skanda of the Bhagavata. It is profusely illustrated and contains the commentary of Sridhara. Every page of the manuscript has pictures illustrative of the narrative. The colours used are permanent and enduring. Krishna leela is depicted with exquisite beauty on many of the pages. There are some pictures like Rasakrida which show the artist at his best in detail and colour. The borders are in gold.

The first 64 inches contain miniature paintings of Ganesa, Saraswathi, Lakshmi-Narayana, Siva, Parvati and the 10 Avataras of Vishnu. At the end paintings of Suka and Parikshit are given. The Skandhas are separated by miniature paintings, besides, there are other small miniatures in between portions of each Skandha. The scroll is very good specimen of calligraphic art. Most of the Manuscripts of the Library collection have been microfilmed. Descriptive catalogues of manuscripts in Sanskrit, Kannada, Marathi have been published.

13

RAMPUR RAZA LIBRARY, RAMPUR

Rampur was a small state but it was very rich in many respects. It contributed a lot to the intellectual and literary world. Such contributions could not be received from larger states as far as the field of knowledge specially music, poetry and education is concerned. The Raza Library of Rampur is the manifestation of such contributions by the rulers of the state.

The Rampur Raza Library is a is very rich in the resources on Indo-Islamic studies and arts. The erstwhile 'Rampur State' later merged with the Indian Union, was founded by Nawab Faizullah Khan in 1774. He ruled over the state up to 1794 and formed the nucleus of the library through his personal collection of valuable manuscripts, historical documents, books and paintings kept in the State's Toshakhana. The Nawabs of Rampur State had been great patrons of renowned scholars, poets, painters, calligraphers and musicians. During the rule of Nawab Ahamd Ali Khan (1794-1840) notable additions to the collections were made. Nawab Muhammad Saeed Khan (1840-55) created a separate Department of the library. He was an enlightened ruler and shifted the collection to new rooms. He appointed Agha Yousuf Ali 'Mahvi' , an Afghan scholar, to organize the collection into a Kutubkhana. The Nawab also invited well–known calligraphers, illuminators and binders from Kashmir and other parts of India.

Nawab Yousuf Ali Khan ascended the throne on First April, 1855. After the historic struggle of 1857, a large number of eminent scholars, poets, writers, musicians, and calligraphers turned towards Rampur and settled here. Nawab Kalbe Ali Khan (1865-87) was very much interested in the collection of rare

manuscripts, paintings etc. He commissioned connoisseur scholars to obtain paintings, illustrated manuscripts, rare books, waslis of famed calligraphers and other art objects and thus enriched the library collection enormously. He travelled abroad and brought a large number of books with him

The next Nawab Mushtaq Ali Khan (1887-89) being disabled, General Azamuddin Khan became Regent of the State in 1887. He formed a managing committee and allocated budget for the maintenance and development of the library. A new building was built and the library collection was shifted from Toshakhana to the new building in 1892. He also opened the library to general public and extended facilities to local academicians and research scholars from other parts of the country. Hundred years back, the staff strength of the library was 50. Nawab Hamid Ali Khan (1889-1930) travelled worldwide before ascending the 'gaddi'. He was highly educated and a patron of art and culture. He was responsible for the construction of impressive palaces, office buildings, markets and pleasure – palaces in Rampur City and its neighbourhood. He constructed a magnificent palace of Indo-European style inside the fort. It was named 'Hamid Manzil' which has been housing the Rampur Raza Library since 1957. He was a connoisseur, added to the collection and introduced certain reforms in management of the library. During his ruling period, Hakim Ajmal Khan, Allama Najmul Ghani Khan and Hafiz Ahmad Ali Khan 'Shauq' managed the library successively

Nawab Raza Ali Khan (1930-66) became the Nawab on 30th June,1930. As he was educated here and abroad, he took unprecedented interest to build the schools and colleges in the State. He was a lover of Indian music for which he purchased several rare manuscripts and books on Indian music. He kept his personal interest in the library affairs after the merger of the State into the Indian Union in December, 1949. He was also responsible for the acquisition of the valuable Loharu Collection of the library. After the independence and the merger of the State in

the Union of India, the Library was brought under the management of a Trust on 6th August, 1951. This Trust management continued till June, 1975. Nawab Murtaza Ali Khan was the President of that Trust. Professor Syed Nurul Hasan, the then Minister of State for Education and Scientific Research, Government of India, visited the library repeatedly and took a serious view of the neglected condition of this priceless heritage. At his instance and Nawab Murtaza Ali Khan, the Government of India took over the library on 1st July, 1975 under the Act enacted by the Parliament and assumed the full central responsibility for the management of the library. Mrs. Indira Gandhi, the Prime Minister, proclaimed the library as an Institution of National importance in a packed meeting ground of the people in her public announcement during her visit to Rampur in 1974.

The Central Government took over the library with effect from 1st July, 1975 under Rampur Raza Library Act (Act No.22 of 1975). The affairs of the library are managed by the Rampur Raza Library Board which has been set up under Section 4 (2) of the Act. It is the governing body with His Excellency, the Hon'ble Governor of Uttar Pradesh as the Chairman. There is a provision of twelve other members including one descendant of the erstwhile ruling Nawab family of Rampur, distinguished historians, scholars in Arabic, Persian and Urdu literature besides officials concerned with the affairs of the library in the Central and State Governments.

Under Section 5 (1) of the Act, Nawab Syed Murtaza Ali Khan was nominated as the Vice-Chairman of the Board for life. After his sad demise on 8th February, 1982, the post of Vice-Chairman lapsed. The post of the Director of the Library is lying vacant since the passing away of Maulana Imtiaz Ali Arshi on 25th February, 1981. As the post of Director / Member Secretary is lying vacant, the Officer On Special Duty is responsible for convening the meetings of the Board and its Sub-Committees and implementation of the decisions taken by the Board. He is

also required to maintain close liaisons with the Chairman of the Board and Department of Culture, Government of India for receiving instructions and regular financial grants for the library

The Rampur Raza Library management is committed to enrich its collection of books, manuscripts, art objects, historical documents, coins through purchases, gifts or exchanges. The devoted Officer On Special Duty leaves no stone unturned in increasing the items of historical importance to the repository of the organization every year.

The library has a newly established and well-organized conservation laboratory which is wedded to the preservation of manuscripts, paintings and art objects. The present Officer On Special Duty is very much concerned about the life of the heritage which may fall a prey to the old time. Due to his life-long experience in the Archaeological Survey of India, he has tried his utmost that the varied problems of the paper must be scientifically encountered, minutely studied and professionally treated with suitable conservation methods.

A large number of scholars, noted litterateurs and dignitaries visit the library regularly. Reputed personalities in the field of literature happened to visit and observe its collections during the 20th century. They have penned down their observations in the visitor's book of the library and rated it as the unique collection richer than those of such other libraries of the world.

Well-known historian and Islamic scholar Allama Shibli Naumani expressed his views and saw the library on 6th April 1914.

"I have consulted this library several times. There is no better collection in India than this. I have also seen the libraries of Egypt, Syria, Turkey and Europe and I can say that this library is richer than any one of them."

Percy Brown, the author of the famous book 'Indian Paintings under the Mughal' has written about the library on 22nd

September 1917. "I have spent a pleasant and most instructive morning in this library with Hafiz Ahmad Ali Khan, the Superintendent as my guide. The pictures have been to me a source of great delight. Some of these are unique.

Collections

Manuscripts

The Raza Library has preserved some rare collections like the seventh century AD Quran written on parchment in early Kufic script attributed to Hazrat Ali. Besides, The library houses a large collection of manuscripts, printed books and miniature paintings. The institution is particularly known for its treasure of Indo-Islamic studies and arts.

In 1975, the Government of India declared the library as an institution of national importance by an act of parliament. Presently, the Raza Library is an autonomous organisation, financed by the Ministry of culture, Government of India.

Housed in two magnificent buildings in the fort of Rampur, the library has a remarkable collection of 15,000 manuscripts, including 150 illustrated ones with 4,413 graphics in them. Besides, there are 205 manuscripts on palm leaves, 1,000 miniature paintings and 1,000 specimens of Islamic calligraphy. The library has more than 50,000 volumes of printed books. It also possesses vast collection of art objects and ancient astronomical instruments. Another feature of the library collection is manuscripts belonging to the libraries of Halb, Makkah, Madinah, Egypt, Iran, Afghanistan and royal libraries of emperors and noblemen.

As per the record of the Library, more than 1,534 scholars from India and abroad visited the library and over 6,048 books and 474 manuscripts were read by them during the year 2000-2001. The library provided 6,866 photographs and 51,211 photocopies of the material to its readers. Besides this, 27,192 visitors came to the library to view and appreciate its collections.

The conservation laboratory has been equipped with modern equipment. The library fumigated 2,624 old printed books, 54 rare Mughal miniature paintings, 525 old manuscripts, 14 old historical documents, 5 big size paintings, 106 old printed books and 26 specimens of calligraphy were conserved and restored.

Raza Library is more famous for its invaluable collection of manuscripts, mostly in Arabic, Persian, Urdu and other Indian languages. The collection of manuscripts as broken up language wise is mentioned below:

Arabic	5,053
Persian	4,060
Urdu	1700
Hidi and Sanskrit	1,000
Tamil	150
Turky and Pushto	50

Arabic

The collection of Arabic manuscripts here is considered as the oldest with rare specimens of Islamic calligraphy and book binding. Among them is the seventh century AD Quran written on parchment in early Kufic script attributed to Hazrat Ali. Another specimen of the holy Quran written in the eighth century AD is attributed to Imam Jafar Sadiq. Another copy of ninth century Quran written on parchment is attributed to Imam Abul Hasan Musa. The celebrated scholar and calligrapher Ibn Muqla, who served three caliphs of Baghdad as prime minister and died on July 20, 941 AD, copied the Quran in the early Naskh style. That masterpiece has found an important place in the collection. The noted calligrapher has reshaped the Arabic letters into Naskh, which is still in vogue in one or the other form. It is a unique specimen of Ibn Muqla's calligraphy.

The library has a copy of the Quran penned by the master calligrapher of the 13th century AD of Baghdad, Yaqut-al Musta'

Simi. It has ornamentation in gold. Another masterpiece of Arabic manuscript by the same calligrapher is Diwan- al- Hadira dated 1221 AD. It was once the part of the royal library of Ibrahim Adil Shah of Bijapur. An interesting work in Arabic of pseudepigraphy and wonderful creations profusely illustrated with strange figures of human beings, animals and birds entitled Ajaibul Makhluqat, was written by Zakaria bin Mahmood al Qazvini (1283 AD) and scripted in elegant Naskh by Ibn Kamaluddin Husain in 1571 AD.

Collection of Persian

The Persian collection comprises of books mainly on Sufism, Medicine, History and literature. The first volume of Tafsir-eTibri is available in the only which is unique in antiquity The other book is Tafseer-e-Zahidi which is considered as a specimen of Persian prose. Three copies of this work are available here. Many copies of Kulliat-eSaidi, Kulliat-eKhusro and Shahnama of Firdausi are available in Library. A book belonging to the period of Firoz Shah is available on Mathmatics entitled Dasturul al Bab fi Ilm-ul Hisaab which is rare.

Zakhirai Khawarizm Shahi is one of the earliest treatises on medicine among the Persian manuscripts of the library. It was scripted by Zainuddin Ibrahim Gurgani (d. 531 AH). Another one is Tafsir-e-Tabri translated from Arabic by Abdul Baqi and scripted by Mirza Muhammad bin Mujtahid in the 12th century AD. It bears the autographs of Shah Abbas of Iran and Qasim Beg Khan in 1621-22 AD. The earliest illustrated Persian work on history of Mongol tribes entitled Jamiul-Tawarikh by Rashidud-Din Fazlullah, includes rare miniatures depicting various aspects of political, social, and religious life of the Mongols. The paintings indicate inspiration of the Chinese and Central Asian early paintings which had influenced the Herat school of painting.

The library has the Khamsa of Nizami Ganjavi (1203 AD) illustrated in 1542-43 AD. It represents the Iranian style and is

beautifully painted against a floral background. The manuscript of the Diwan-i-Jami bears a beautiful seal of Hamida Bano Begum, daughter of Ali Akbar, mother of emperor Akbar and that of Nazar Ara, daughter of Shah Jahan, on the colophon. It is interesting to note that Nazar Ara Begum, whose seal appears on the colophon, does not appear to be mentioned in the contemporary Persian literature. Diwan-i-Hafiz, a rare illustrated manuscript, is among the collections of the library. It was written in Akbar's eventful reign around 1570-80 AD, and was illustrated by celebrated court painters.

Among the other rare Persian manuscripts of the library there is a copy of Risalah Khawaja Abdullah Ansari and Sad Pand-i-Luqman bound together and scribed in elegant Nastaliq by the master calligrapher Mir Ali of Herat, who died in 1544 AD. It bears signatures and seals of several kings and scholars and was graded as being of first category by emperor Shah Jahan and was purchased by him for Rs 1,000. He presented another copy of the same Risalah to Jahan Ara Begum who lavishly praised its importance in her own handwriting in 1588 AD and bears the seals of Shah Jahan and Aurangzeb.

A unique illustrated Ramayan of Valmiki translated into Persian by Sumer Chand and illustrated during the reign of Farrukh Siyar in 1715-16 AD bears 258 miniatures throwing light on the art, architecture, costumes and ornaments of the period, besides highlighting the composite culture of India in the late medieval period.

Urdu Books

Urdu books are less in number compared to the Persian and Arabic collections but they are equally important They include Diwas Zada Shah Alam, Kulliate Sauda, Kulliat-eHasan, Diwan-eSouz and Diwan-eGhalib. Two copies of Rani Ketki by Insha are also available in the Library which have been the basis for writing the story in correct form. The collection also include the copy of Diwan of Mirza Ghalib which he presented to the Nawab as a gift before 1857.

Apart from the books in Arabic Persian and Urdu a number of valuable works are available 9n other languages also mainly Hindi, Sanskrit, Tamil, Turkey and Pushto.

Collection of Palm Leaves

The collection of palm leaf manuscripts is among the valuable assets of Raza Library. Most of them are in Telugu, Sanskrit, Kannada, Sinhala or Tamil. They are generally religious in character. A Tamil script mentions the rules of preparing images and icons and the mode of worship; another leaf manuscript tells the medicinal properties of herbs. One such manuscript in Sanskrit written in Grantha script; is of the Ramayan. It eulogises the Ramayan as Brhahmavachakam. A Kannada manuscript is a treatise on music and yet another manuscript is Periyatine Vaimoli, the sacred hymn of the Vaishnavas. Besides manuscripts and books, the library is also a treasure-trove of antique art objects and rare astronomical instruments. The oldest instrument of the collection is an astrolabe made by Siraj Damashqi in 1218 AD. The instrument was used for measuring the latitude of the sun and stars for navigational purposes and astronomy. Two other astrolabes by the same instrument maker are dated back to 1225 AD and 1230 AD and are found in the collections of Salar Jung Museum, Hyderabad, and National Museum, New Delhi. Apart from these, the Raza library has a vast collection of books in Sanskirt, Turkish, Pushto, Hindi, Urdu and other languages.

14
SALAR JUNG MUSEUM AND LIBRARY, HYDERABAD

The Salar Jung Museum of Hyderabad is the repository of the artistic achievements of diverse European, Asian and Far Eastern countries of the world. The major portion of this collection was acquired by Mir Yousuf Ali Khan popularly known as Salar Jung III, but quite a few items were inherited by him from his father Nawab Mir Laiq Ali Khan Salar Jung II and his grand father Nawab Mir Turab Ali Khan, Sir Salar Jung I .

This eclectic treasure of world art of over 40,000 objects has grown out of the rich and variegated collection acquired by them but more specifically by Mir Yusuf Ali Khan, popularly known as Salar Jung III (1889-1949).

He served briefly as Prime Minister (from 1912-14) to Mir Osman Ali Khan, the seventh Nizam of Hyderabad. He spent a considerable portion of his wealth in collecting objects of art and other curios in staggering profusion. He was indeed a consummate dilettante and a shrewd connoisseur of everything pertaining to art & antiquities, as the collection in the museum testifies.

After his death, in the absence of any direct descendents, the Indian Government appointed a committee to administer the Salar Jung Estate. To perpetuate the name of Salar Jung, a private museum of that name came into being in December 1951, in the Diwan Deodi, the ancestral palace of Salar Jung III. It was declared open by the first Prime Minister of India, Pundit Jawaharlal Nehru. The control and supervision of the Salar Jung Estate was fully passed to the Indian Government in 1960 and

for a year the Museum was administered directly by the Ministry of Scientific Research & Cultural Affairs. By an Act of Parliament , known as the Salar Jung Museum Act, 1961, the Museum with the Library were declared to be an "Institution of National Importance."

The Museum then shifted to it's present premises in 1968, and was declared open by Dr. Zakir Hussain. Under the Salar Jung Museum Act of 1961, the Indian government transferred the administration of the Museum on July 1, 1961 to a Board of Trustees with the Governor of Andhra Pradesh as ex-officio Chairperson.

The Salar Jung Museum Act has empowered the Board of Trustees, which is an autonomous body, not only to manage the Museum efficiently, but also to plan, promote, organize and implement programs for the proper development of the Museum. Moreover the Board has been fully authorized to take such measures, as it thinks fit for providing instruction and research in activities bearing on museums & libraries, and for the advancement of learning.

Salar Jung museum is the fantasy of an art visionary come to life which waited for its consummation for another great lover of art Jawaharlal Nehru to visit the historic city of the Quli Qutab Shahs and inaugurate it on 16 December, 1951 when the collections were hurriedly assorted and housed in Diwan Devdi, residence of the Salar Jungs. Every year a million visitors pay homage to this great repository of art and history. The priceless collections were moved in 1968 to a new site from the 100-year-old palace Dewan Devdi of the prime ministers. Legend has that the museum houses art collections of three generations of the Salar Jung family, beginning with Salar Jung, who was prime minister under...

The incomparable treasures of the museum, consisting only of a part of the original collection, are an amazing amalgam of antiquity and modernity, the three Salar Jungs scouring continents for objets d'art and returning home with shiploads of artefacts.

It is believed that during the colonial period a lot of the art wealth of the country was shipped to the metropolitan countries and the Salar Jungs are credited with bringing back some of it to enrich the collection. The museum represents, in popular belief, the largest one-man collections of the world. They reflect the stunning range of time and place of these treasures, some of them belonging to different civilisations and dating back to the first century and retrieved from nearly every nook and corner of the world. However, the chief architect of this great and magnificent congeries of art is believed to be Salar Jung III, i.e. Nawab Mir Yusuf Ali khan.

The marvellous expose unveils the art heritage of India, Asia, Middle East and Europe and includes Persian carpets, Chinese porcelain, Japanese lacquer ware, sculpture, invaluable collections of jade, bronzes, enamelware, paintings, wood and inlay work from Tibet, Nepal and Thailand etc. There are Aurangzeb's sword, daggers belonging to empress Noor Jehan, emperors Jehangir and Shah Jehan, the turbans and chair of Tippu Sultan, furniture from Egypt, paintings etc. Among the sculptures stands out the world famous statue of Veiled Rebecca, her beautiful face hazily visible through; hold your breath, a marble but gossamer veil. The visitor may mistake it for a gorgeous woman draped in a wet garment. Equally captivating is a double-figure wood sculpture done by G.H. Benzoni, an Italian sculptor, in 1876. It stands before a mirror and shows the facade of a nonchalant Mephistopheles and the image of a demure Margaretta in the mirror.

A bewildering variety and array of clocks greets the visitor in the clock room. Seen are the ancient Sandiaers in the form of obelisks to huge and modern clocks of the twentieth century. Others in the range vary from miniature clocks which need a magnifying glass to imbibe their beauty and complexity to stately grandfather clocks from as far away as France, Germany, Italy, Switzerland and Britain. A visual delight is the musical clock Salar Jung bought from Cook and Kelvy of England, a virtual

mechanical marvel. Every hour, a timekeeper emerges from the upper deck of the clock to strike a gong as many times as it is the hour of the day.

Stunning is the jade room or gallery hosting items articulating the delicateness and elegance of jade, which is not found in India and believed to have been introduced during the Mughal rule. Though the stone is imported, the articles of jade on display in the gallery were all the handiwork of Indian artists. Jade, soft and lucent, was carved into handles for small daggers studded with precious stones and inlay work. A jade wine bowl you can see here is a thing of beauty, dainty and transparent. Also striking are the wine cups made of jade with leaf and flower motifs. You can also see small and cute jade platters which at one time adorned the dining tables of the Salar Jungs.The jade collection also includes a jade stand of Altamash (1209-10 A.D); fruit knife of Mughal empress Noorjehan (17th century); hunting knife of emperor Jehangir; an inscribed archery ring of emperor Shah Jehan done in dark green jade (17th century).

The textile gallery is a depository of Indian textile art in cotton, silk and wool, dominated by a collection of brocades woven with silver and gold thread and the world-famous Kashmiri shawls. Gold and zari add to the value of the embroidery, which showcases also phulkari embroidery work from Punjab. An entire rich and brick-coloured cotton expanse disappears behind a fine façade of intricately woven silk thread in a burst of colours.

A special feature is the glassware from England, Austria, Ireland, France, Belgium, Czechoslovakia and Turkey besides glassware belonging to Ming and Ching periods. There is the Ivory Room resplendent with intricately carved items and articles among which worthy of mention are chess sets, statuettes, painted objects done by using the cutaway technique. About the technique an article appearing in the Hindustan Times says, "Here the ivory is first carved with a lacy surface design. The space behind it is cut away till the design shows up like a screen. And further carving continues at deeper levels of the ivory. The object then

acquires a trellis-like case and the forms within forms are created out of a single piece of ivory."

Every form of art in its ancient glory finds its representation in the museum. Statuary includes a standing Buddha image of limestone from Nelakondapalli (2nd or 3rd century A.D.); Mukhalinga from Kausambi (4th or 5th century A.D.); Ananthasayi Vishnu with his ten avatars carved on top (12th century A.D., Kakatiyaa, Warangal); Jain, Buddhist and Hindu bronzes dating back to later Pallava and Chola periods and the two most famous exhibits of the museum – the Veiled Rebecca and a sycamore wood carwing portraying a double statue of Mephistopheles and Margaretta. The mammoth collection includes paintings such as "Soap Bubbles" by Fransesco Hayez of Italy; "Piazzo of San Marco" by Antonio Canaletto (1697-1768) and "Venice" by Marc Aldine of Italy. Pottery items range from Dresden (Germany), Sevres (France), Capodimonte (Italy) to Wedgewood and English porcelain.

In short, the museum is a standing monument to the artistic genious of mankind throughout the space-time spectrum.

LIBRARY

Books

The museum is home to 43,000 art exhibits and 50,000 books collected from all over the world. Old timers believe that the present collection constitutes only half of the original art wealth amassed by Salar Jung III. His employees siphoned off part of it, since Salar Jung was a bachelor and depended upon his staff to keep a vigil. Some more art pieces were lost or stolen during the shifting of the museum from Dewan Devdi to the present site. The museum, declared an institution of national importance by an Act of Parliament in 1961, overlooks another landmark, the languid Musi, of the four hundred-year-old city founded by Mohammed Quli Qutub Shah. This great treasure trove is a tribute to man's eternal quest for beauty and elegance, particularly India's remarkable cultural diversity and heritage.

The library collection is very rich in histories, biographies ornate prose and official letters and documents which through light on the political and cultural life of the Deccan from the 17th to the 19th centuries. Some of the works are very rare indeed.

Other attractions are a gallery exclusively devoted to the celebrated family of the Salar Jungs, a children's section, a reference library and a section devoted to rare and ancient Arabic Urdu and Persian manuscripts, including a handwritten miniature Qoran. On display are unique mementos like the panegyric in Urdu presented to Sir Salar Jung and Nizam VI in memory of their visit to Delhi to witness the Imperial Proclamation of Queen Victoria in 1877. The first room houses the personal items of the Salar Jung household such as various mementoes received by the Salar Jungs, embroidered sherwanis and a commodious and arresting masnad (ceremonial throne-like chair used by Salar Jung III). In the room, one can also see a large portrait of Mir Yousuf Khan, the clothes of the nobility, their books and furniture and bric-a-brac.

Walking through the museum is walking through the ages of several civilisations, Indus, Egyptian, Mesopotamian, Roman to name a few and is bound to disengage the visitor from the present, the current and the immediate and transport him to a world he is familiar with only through reading. Throughout your trek through the endless halls, rooms, galleries and corridors of the museum, you are in a daze.

In the field of poetry also the Library is very rich. It contains about 1200 manuscripts which are catalogued n three volumes: IV to VI A good few Diwaans and anthologies are extremely rare and valuable. A wealth of information is available for research scholars.

Manuscripts

The Library contains 7,742 manuscripts out of which 4,146 are in Persian. This collection is one of the ppremier private treasures in India which ranks next to the great oriental

manuscripts libraries and serves as an auxiliary to the Khuda Bakhsh Library, Patna, The National Library, The Asiatic Society Library, Calcutta and other important oriental collections in India and elsewhere.

The following is the number of manuscripts available in the Library

Persian	4,146
Arabic	2,459
Urdu	1,045
Hindi	2,000

The following works deserve special mention and the Library is proud to own them:

1. Ta'rikh-e-Qutub shahi by Khurshah b. Quḅad al-Husaini c97/565 is the general history of the World compiled by Ibrahim Qutub Shah of Golconda 57-89/55-. It is a Royal copy. An other known copy of this work is in the British Museum.
2. Tajul Maasir. A history of the Early Sultans of Delhi 1191-1217. It is the oldest known copy having been transcribed in 1325.
3. Shah Jahanama. It is the history of the first ten years of rein of shah Jahan. An imperial copy written in excellent nastaliq on gold sprinkled paper. The authors name in not known. It appears to be the only known copy.
4. Shahinsha nama-e- Shah Jahan. A collection of prose and poetry pertaining to the life of the Mughal emperopr. It is the only knpown copy.
5. Mirat-e-Sadiq by Mohammad /Shafia Wearid c1736. Is is the history of Mughal India written as an appendix to Farishta's gulshan-eIbrahimi. It is the only known copy in existence.
6. Tabsira-e Ulin-nuhạ, by Mir Mohammad Ahsan entitled Ma'ni Yab Khan. A history of Farrukhsiyar's reign that

throughs light on the condition of the country on those troublesome days. The other known copy is in the British Mnuseum.

7. Tadhkira-e Asifiya. It is the history of first three Nizams by Vir Rai, the Chronicler who gives detailed account of those days as he found them. It is the inly copy available.
8. Tarikh-eMahabat Jung. An anonymous compilation of the history of Bengal under Aliwardy Khan Mahabat Jung. It is a rare work.
9. Mah Nama c 1814. A history of the Nizams of Hyderabad written for Mahlaqa Bai the favourate courtisan of Asif Jah II. The copy was transcribed five years after it was compiled.
10. Beklarnama. A history of Sindh compiled for Capt. Stock of East India company.

A catalogue for Arabic and Persian manuscripts was planned to be brought in 20 volumes representing the following subjects in each language;

Catalogue of Arabic Manuscripts

I. Philosophy, Logic. Theology etc

II. Holy Quran. Fragments, Commentaries etc

III. Principles of Tradition, Jurisprudence, Fiqh, Fatawa of all Sunni Scholls etc.

IV. Principles of Tradition, Jurisprudence, Fiqh, Fatawa of all Shia Schools etc.

V. Sifism, Homiletics, Preaching etc.

VI. Philosophy, Literature, Poetry and Prose and Biography of Poets

VII. Mathematics, Astronomy, Chemistry, Useful Arts, Secret Arts, Fine Arts, Medicine etc.

VIII. Geography, History, Biography, Compendiums.

Catalogue of Persian Mnauscripts

I. Philosophy, Logic. Theology etc.

II. Quranic Science , Recitation, Translations, Commentaries, Traditions, Law of all Schools.

III. Sufism, Ethics, Homiletics, Prayers and Preachings and Biographies of Sufies.

IV. Mathematics, Astronomy, Chemistry, Secret Arts, Useful Arts, Fine Arts et.

V. Medicine Vetenary Science etc.

VI. Lexicon, Grammar,, rhetoric, Prosody, etc

VII. Poetry

VIII. Poetry

IX. Biographies of Poets, Prose Works, etc.

X. Geography, History, Biographies Works of Mixed Contents and Miscellany.

XI. Geography, History, Biographies, Works of Mixed Contents and Miscellany.

The manuscripts have immense value for the lovers of arts and learnings and scholars devoted to the study of Eastern civilization, history, philosophy, religion, literatyre and culture of the Asian people embedded in Arabic Persian and Indian languages.

The collectin abounds in several antiquities, relics of Asian countries, masterpieces of Asian arts and learning, works of great thinkers, artists and unique specimenof book-arts collected from various Islamic countries of the Middle East. The rarities present various apochs, styles, schools and centres patronage and show the development of the art of calligraphy, miniature painting, decoration and illumination, gliding, binding, papermaking and prepararion of ink of all colours.

The special feature of the collection is that it is rich in de-luxe Codexes of the Holy Quran representing Muslim Calligraphy at its highesyt from the 8th to 18th century A.D. It also containd

genuine manuscripts and autograph copies of royal and historical personags and famous calligraphers like Yaqut-I-Must'asimi. The rarities of the collection may be grouped as under:

1. Manuscripts of unique, original and highly intrinsic literary and historical value hitherto unknown.
2. Rare works as well as material for research produced by distinguished authors and compilers.
3. Works of contemporaneous value, containing accurate and reliable texts.
4. Works containing special external features, e.g. records of ownership, endorsement, autographs, seals of special owners, collections and libraries, and colophons bearing the date, place and name of the scribe etc.
5. Works of artistic value bearing calligraphic and other decorative features mentioned below.
6. Other manuscripts of outstanding value from the intrinsic and extraneous point of view.

The cata logue of the manuscripts provide brief description of each manuscript in order to reveal the author, title external features, and bibliographical information at a glance for the researchers. Entries are araanged alphabetically under each subjects as mentioned above. The main object is to acquint scholars working on several Islamic subjects in different countries with the real nature and content of the Collection.

15
SURVEY OF ORIENTAL COLLECTIONS

The Indira Gandhi National Centre for the Arts, New Delhi took an initiative to list the Oriental libraries and specially manuscripts available in them in different languages. In 1999, they came out with a detailed list of the institutions containing the Oriental collections. The list covers the libraries state wise and can be taken as the most comprehensive work in surveying of the Oriental manuscripts in the country so far.

Andhra Pradesh

Hyderabad	Andhra Pradesh Govt. Oriental Mss. Lib. and Research Institute
Tirupati	Sri Venkateswar oriental REs. Institute
Hyderabad	Salar jung Museum Liberary
Hyderabad	Kutub Khana-I-Saidiya
Hyderabad	Jamia Nizamia
Hyderabad	Abul Kalam Azad Oriental Res. Institute
Hyderabad	Archival Cell (Dept. of History)
Hyderabad	Birla Archaeological and Cultural Res. Inst
Hyderabad	City Central Library
Hyderabad	Osmania University Regional Library
Rajahmundry	Sri Gowthami Regional Library
Rajahmundry	Sri Rallabandhi Subbarao Archeological Museum
Vishakhapatanam (Waltair)	Andhra University Library, Dr. V S Krishma Library

Rajahmundry	Andhra Historical Research Society
Vishakjpatanam	Arsha Library
Hyderabad	Oriental Public Bureau and Dairat Ul Maarif
Chitoor	Samskrita Bhasha Pracharini Sabha
Kakinada (Ramraspet)	Telugu Academy
Hyderabad	Sanskrit Academy, Osmania University
Hyderabad	Henery martyn Institute of Islamic Studies
Hyderabad	The state Archieves of Andhrapradesh
Bhattanavalli	The sanskrit press and Publications
Aukiripalli, Krishna	Sri Markandeya Sanskrit College
Guntur	Sri Sharada Niketanam
Vijayanagaram	Maharaja's Govt. Sanskrit College
Nellore	Veda and Sanskrit College
Tirumala	T T D Veda Pathashala
Vetapalem	Saraswata Niketan
Vizianagaram	The Vizianagaram Fort
Assam	
Nalabari	Kamarupa Sanskrit Sanjivani Sabha
Nalabari	Nalabari Sanskrit College
Nalabari	Purva bharati
Guahati	Narayani Handiqui Historical Institute (Dept. of History & Antiquarain Studies
Guahati	Kamarupa Anusandhana Samiti
Guahati	Guahati University
Navagradham	Pragjyotishpur Sanskrit Vidhyapith
Bihar	
Patna	Khuda Baksh Ori. pub. Library
Patna	Bihar & Orissa Research Society

Patna	Madarasa Islamia Shamsul Huda
Vaishali, Muzafarpur	Mithila Research Institute
Darbhanga	Chandradhari Museum
Patna	Patna University Library
Vaishali	Pali Research Institute
Mongher	Jamia Rahmaniya
Patna	Dept. of History, Patna University
Patna	Dept. of Persian, Patna University
Patna	K P Jayswal Research Institute
Darbhanga	The Laksmiswar public Library
Bhagalpur	Mandar Vidhapeeth
Darbhanga	Mithila Inst. of post Graduate Studies and Research in Sanskrit Learning
Nalanda	Navanalanda Mahavihar (Magadh University)
Darbhanga	Darul Uloom Ahmadiya Salafia
Katihar	Darul Uloom latif
Darbhanga	Kameswar Singh Darbanga Sanskrit University
Patna	Bihar State Central Library (Srimati Radhika Devi Res. Inst)
Bhagalpur	Bhagavan Pustakalaya
Arrah	Sri Dev Kumar Jai Oriental Research Inst.
Begusarai	Ganesh Dutta College
Delhi	
New Delhi	National Archieves
New Delhi	Indian Council of Cultural Relation, Azad Bhawan.
New Delhi	National Museum
Delhi	Delhi Archieves

New Delhi	Delhi University Library
New Delhi	ICSSR, Social Science Documentation Centre
New Delhi	Indian Institute of Islamic Studies
New Delhi	Raja Rammohan Roy National Educational Resources Centre Library
New Delhi	Sri Ram Centre for Indusrial Relations & Human Resources Library
Delhi	Mahabir Jain Pustakalaya
Delhi, Timarpur	Bharatiya Vidya Sansthan (Inst. of Indology)
Delhi	Madarsa Aminiya
New Delhi	Dr. Zakir Husain Library (Jamia Milia Islamia)
New Delhi	International Academy of Indian Culture, Haus Khas Enclave
Alipur, Delhi	Bhogilal Lehrchand Research Institute
Delhi	Dargah hazrat Shah Abul Khair
New Delhi, Nizamuddin	Galib Academy
Goa	
Portogal, Goa	Gomantak Sanskritottejak Mandal's Sanskrit Pathasala, Portogal Swami's Library
Keri	Gomantak Sasnkrit Parishad
Panji	Cental Library
Gujarat	
Ahmedabad	Mahrsi Academy of Vedic Sciences
Ahmedabad	Sheth Bholabhai Jseinghbhai Institute of Learning and Research
Dwarka	Shri Dwarkadhist Sanskrit Academy and

	Indological Research Institute
Patan	Sri Hemchandra jain Gyan Mandir
Gandihnagar	Sri Mahavir Jain Aradhana Kendra
Ahmedabad	Hazrat Pir- Muhammad Shah Dargah Library
Anand	Jamia Arabia Talimul Islam
Baroda	Oriental Institute
Ahmedabad	B J Institute of Learning and Research
Vallabh Vidhyanar	Sardar Patel Unversity
Baroda	Baroda Sanskrit mahavidhyalaya
Cambey	Jain Bhandaras
Limbadi	Jain Bhandars
Chhani	Jain Bhandars
Baroda	Atmanada Jnana Mandir
Baroda	Jain Jnana Mandir
Baroda	Arya jambuswami Jain Muktabai Jnana Ashram
Ahmedabad	L.D.Institute (L.D.Bharatiya Sanskriti Vidyamandir)
Ahmedabad	Gujrat Vidyapith Library
Ahmedabad	Patana Jain Bhandara
Ahmedabad	Gujrat Vidya Sabha
Ahmedabad	University School of Languages, Gujrat University
Ahmedabad	The Brahmachari Wadi
Vhani, Baroda	The Jain Swetamber Jnana Mandir
Rajkot	Saurashtra Research Society
Pardi	Swadhyaya Mandala and Vedic Research Institute
Bhavnagar	Vashovijaya Jain Granthamala

Gondal	Bhubaneswari Vidhyapith
Surat	Jamia Saitiya
Ahmedabad	Darul Uloom Shah Alam
Vaduvan	Acharya Maharaj Sri Swaminarayan Mandir
Dakore	Dakore Temple Committee
Junagarh	Narasingh Mehta Chopra Trust
Vaniavada, Mota Deka, Bhuj	Sri Jain Swetamber Murtipujak Tapgacch Sangh
Surenderanagar	Sri Swaminarayan Temple
Porbander	Sudama Temple
Haryana	
Rohtak	Gurkul Jhajhar Haryana Prantiya Puratatwa Sanghrahalaya
Rohtak	Dayanand Vedic Santhan Gurukul, Singhpura
Kurukshetra	Sanatan Dharma Pathasala
Kurukshtra	Kurukshetra University Library
Himachal Pradesh	
Mandi	Himachal Lok Sanskriti Samsthan
Shimla	Himachal Academy of Arts Culture and Languages, sngarmal Bhawan
Shimla	Samskrita Shodha Samsthan, divyajyoti
Nahan, Sirmur	The Govt. District Library
Kangra	Mata Sri Vrajesweri Devi Mandir Trust
Jammu & Kashmir	
Jammu	Sri Ran. Skt. Res. Institute
Srinagar	Research and Publication Department, JK Govt.
Srinagar	State Archives Dept. Govt. of J & K.

Srinagar	Sri Rupa Devi Sharda Peeth
Srinagar	Directorate of Library, Museum and Rearch
Srinagar	The Shadapith Research Centre
Srinagar	Kashmir University, Ikbal Library

Karnataka

Hubli	S.J.M.Math
Dharmshala	Jai Basadi Moodbidri
Mangalagangotri	Mangalore University Library
Bangalore	Central Power Research Institute Library
Dharwad	Karnataka Historical Research Society
Melkote	Academy of Sanskrit Research
Moodbidri	Sri Vira Vani Vilasa Jain Sinddhanta Bhawan
Moodbidri	The Danasala Matha Sastra Bhandara
Bangalore	Sri Chamarajendra Sanskrit College Chamrajpeth
Tumkur	Sri Siddhanlingeswer Sanskrit Colege and Veda Pathsala, Siddhanganga
Melkote, Pandavapura	Sanskrit College, Manday
Mysore	The Parakala Mutt Library
Udipi	M G M College
Udipi	Mutt of Sri Madhvacharya Sansthan
Karkala	Jaina Mutt
Udipi	Sri Krishna Mutt
Udipi	The Pejawar Mutt
Mysore	The Palace saraswati Bhandar, Maha. Skt Coll.
Sravanavelagola	Srimaccarukirti Panditacarya Jain Bhandar

Sringeri	The Sharada Pitha. The Mutt H.H. Swami
Sringeri	Sankara Narayana Jyautisika
Bangalore	Kannada Sahitya Parishat
Mysore	Maharaja Sanskrit College
Mysore	Mysore Sanskrit Academy
Udupi	S M S P Sanskrit College
Melkote	Vedavedantebodhini Sanskrit College
Dharwad	Karnataka University, Dept. of Skt, History (Post graduate teaching)
Gulbara	Institute of Kannada Studies (Gulbara University)
Dharwad	Institute of Kanada Studies (University of Karnakta)
Bangalore	Bangalore University Library
Bangalore	Kalpataru Research Academy
Dharmasthala	Sri Manjunatheswar Cultural & Research Institute
Dharwar	Vidyadhisha Sanskrit manuscript Library
Mysore	Oriental Research Institute
Bangalore	United Theological College
Kerala	
Keladi	Keladi Museum & H R B
Trivandrum	O. R. I & Messs. Library
Trivandrum	The state Archieves of Kerala
Tripunithura	Sri Ram Verma Govt. Skt. College
Cochin	Central Inst. of Fisheries Techno. Library
Trichur	Rama Verma Research Institute, Town Hall
Kasaragod	Edneermath
Kottayam	Kottayam Public Library

Calicut	Manuscript Library (Deptt, of Malayalam) University of Calicut
Calicut	Calicut University Library
Palghat	Chandraprabha Digambara Jain Basti
Thiruvanantapuram	Kerala Granthasala Sandham
Palghat	Palghat educational & Cultural Council
Madhya Pradesh	
Ujjain	Scindia Ori. Res. Institute
Bhopal	Darul Uloom Tajul Masjid
Bhopal	Jamia Islamia Arabia
Rewa	Avadesh Pratapsingh University (Mahakavi Kesav Adhyayan evam Anusandhan Kendra
Bhopal	Directorate of Archaeology and Museums
Indore	Public Library, Govt. sanskrit College
Indore	Central Museum
Datia	Govt. Sanskrit College
Chattarpur	Palace Library
Panna and Rewa	Private Libraries of Maharajas
Laskar	Narayan Sikshia Samiti
Nagod, Satna	Public Library
Panna	Prannath Mandir
Rewa	Vyankent Vidya Sadan Library
Datia	Sri Peetambara Peetha
Gawalior	Matrubhumi Karyalaya
Bhopal	Prachya Niketan (Centre of Advance studies in indology and musology)
Bhopal	Hindi Bhawan, Motilal Nehru Smarak Pustakalaya
Gawalior	Jiwaji University Library

Impahal	Natum Sangeet Academy
Impahal	Guru S. K. S. Collection
Impahal	Y. D. S Collection
Impahal	Manipur State Kala Academy
Impahal	Atombapu Res Centre
Impahal	Pt. N.K.S. Collection
Impahal	Manipur State Archives
Impahal	Manipur State Museum
Impahal	Hijam Romani Singh Collection
Impahal	Mutua Museum
Kanchipuram	Sri Kanchi Sankar Math
Kakching, Mani.	People's Museum
Impahal	Manipuri Sahitya Parishad
Impahal	Thangjam Chandra Singh Research Library

Maharashtra

Nagpur	Nagpur University Library
Pune	Bharata Itihasa Samsodhaka Mandala
Pune	Anandashram Sanstha
Pune	Bhandarkar Ori. Res. Institute
Pune	Vaidika Samsodhan Mandala
Mumbai	Jama Masjid Trust Library
Mumbai	Asiatic Society
Mumbai	Bombay University
Mumbai	Maharastra State Archieves
Kohlapur	Shivaji Universiry (BARR) Balasaheb Khandekar Library
Poona	Poona Universiry, Laykar Library
Mumbai	Smt. Nathi Bai Damodar Thakarsey women's University Library

Nagpur	Anthropological Survey of India LIbrary (Central)
Pune	The Mandalik Library, Fergussion College
Nasik	The Hamsaraj Pragji Thakersey College
Raipur	Rajpur Sanskrit Pathsala
Nagpur	Jamia Arabia Islamia
Bombay (Colaba)	Anantacharya Indolofical Research Institute
Bombay	Bhartiya Vidya Bhawan
Bombay	Bhartiya vidya Bhawan
Shirur	Vhandmal Tarachand Bora College
Beed (Ambajogai)	Dasopant Samsodhan Mandal
Pune	Deccan College Post Graduate & Research Institute
Nasik	HPT Arts & RYK Science College
Thane	Institute for Oriental studies
Dhule	IBK Rajwade Samsodhan Mandal
Bombay	KR Cama Oriental Institute
Yavatmal, Arni Road	Shardashram
Amravati	Sri Samrthi Vagdevata Mandir
Dhule	Sri Samarthi Vagdevata Mandir
Mumbai	Asiatic Society of Bombay
Nagpur	The Bhonsala Veda Shastra Mahavidyalaya
Yeotmal	C P andBerar Jain Research Institute
Mumbai	Forbes Gujarati Sabha, Vithalbhai Patel Rd.
Mumbai	Heras Institute of India History and Culture, St. Xavier's college
Mumbai	Marathi Samsodhan Mandal, marathi grantha Sangrahalaua. Thakurdwar

Dhulia	Rajwade Samsodhan Mandal
Rajpur, Ratnagiri	Sanskrit Pathshala
Ahmednagar	Sanatan Dharma Sabha
Fort Bombay	Secretatiat Record Office, Elphistone College building
Pune	Vedasastrottejaka Sabha, sdasiva peth
Nagpur	Vidarbha Sahitya Samgam
Ahmednagar	Darul Uloom
Pune	French Prachya Vidya Mandir
Mumbai	Anjuma-i-Islam Urdu Research Institute
Mumbai	Centre for Education and Documentation Library
Wai	Prajna Pathashala
Mumbai	Princes of Wales Museum and Western India
Pune	Tilak Maharastra vidyapith
Orissa	
Bhubaneswar	Orissa State Museum
Bhubaneswar	Utkal University Parija Library
Berhmpur	Archival Cell (Berhempur University)
Berhmpur	Archival Cell (Berhempur university)
Bhubaneswar	Kedarnath Gaveshana Pratisthan
Berhmpur, Tulsinagar	Literacy Home
Balangir	Vidyabhushan Sanskrit College
Puri	Jagannath Aitihasika Gaveshana Samiti and raghunandan Library
Bhubaneswar	Orissa State Archives
Puri	Sadasiva sanskrit College
Paralakhemundi, Ganj	Paralakhemundi Sanskrit college

Naugao (Udaipur)	Sri Aurovindo Sangrahalaya
Cuttack (Udaipur)	Sri Aurovindo Sangrahalaya
Pondicherry	
Pondicherry	Aurovindo Ashram
Pondicherry	Paventher Bharathidasan Memorial cum
Pondicherry	Romain Rolland Library
Punjab	
Hoshiarpur	V.V.R.I
Amritsar	Guru Nanak Dev University Library
Amritsar	Central Sikh Museum (Golden Temple)
Chandigarh	Punjab University, Dept. of Punjabi
Patiala	Punjab State Archieves
Amritsar	Khalsa College Library
Hoshiarpur	VVRI of Sanskrit & Indological studies (Punjab University)
Rajasthan	
Alwar	Govt. State Museum
Jaipur,citypalace	Sawai Mansingh II Museum
Jaipur	Digambara Jain Nasiyan Bhattarkijji
Tonk	Arabic & Persian Res. Institute
Jodhpur	Rajasthan Oriental Research Institute
Udaipur	Rajasthan Oriental Research Institute
Udaipur	Rajasthan Oriental Research Institute
Bikaner	Rajasthan Oriental Research Institute
Chittorgarh	Rajasthan Oriental Research Institute
Jaipur	Rajasthan Oriental Research Institute
Alwar	Rajasthan Oriental Research Institute
Kota	Rajasthan Oriental Research Institute
Udaipur	Rajasthan Oriental Research Institute

Bharatpur	Rajasthan Oriental Research Institute
Chaupasani, Jodhpur	Rajasthani Sodha Samsthan
Udaipur	State Museum
Jaipur (city)	Dadu Mahavidyalaya
Jaipur	Digamber Jain Sanskrit College
Jaipur	Madhusudan Vaidik Vijnana Prakashak Karyalaya
Bikaner	Rajasthan State Archives
Bikaner	Shardul Sanskrit Vidyalaya, rani bazar
Tonk	Rajasthan Oriental Research Institute
Tonk	Darul Uloom Khalilliya Nizamiya
Bikaner	Anup Sanskrit Library
Bikaner	Bharatiya Vidyamandir Shodh Pratisthan
Bikaner	Hindi Viswa Bharati Anusandhan Parishad
Ladun	Jain Viswa Bharati
Churu	Lok Sanskriti Sadh Sansthan
Jodhpur	Maharaj Mansingh Pustak Pakash
Ajmer	Paropakarini Sabha
Borunda	Rupayam Sansthan
Jodhpur	Sewa Mandir
Bharatpur	Shri Hindi Sahitya Samiti
Sikar	Shri Mahavir Pustakalaya
Jodhpur	The Archaeological Dept. of Jodhpur state
Mewar	The Saraswati Bhandar Library
Jaipur	The Prachya Vidhya Pratisthan
Udaipur	The Sajjan Vanivilas Library
Udaipur	The Library of Nathadwara
Jaipur	Sri Ram Charan Museum
Banasthali	Vanasthali Vidyapith

Tamilnadu

Chennai	Govt. Oriental Mss. Library
Chennai	Dr. U.V.S.I. Library
Chennai	Ramakrishna Mission
Thanjavur	TMSSM Library
Chennai	Kingdom of Trivandrum
Kanchipuram	Kingdom of Trivandrum
Madurai	Saurashtra Sabha
Chennai	Kupuswami Sastri Res. Institute
Chennai	Adyar Library and Research Centre
Annamalai Nagar	Annamalai University Library
Thanjavur	Tamil University (Dept. of epigraphy)
Thanjavur	Tamil University (Dept. of His. & rare paper Mss.)
Thanjavur	Tamil University (Dept. of Palam leaf Mss.)
Madurai	Govt. Museum
Chennai	Institute of Asian Studies
Kanchipuram	Madurai Province Jesuit Archives
Shrothium Navalpakkam	Nyaya Mimamsa Anusandhan Kendra
Madurai	Madurai Kamraj University
Shrotium Navalpakkam	Sri Hayagriva Mahala Library
Thanjavur	Karandai Tamil Samgam
Mayauram	Vasudeva Brahmendra Saraswati Library
Madurantakam	Ahobila Mutt Sanskrit College
Madurai	The Rameswaram Devasthanam Pathasala
Kanchi Conjivaram	The Upanishad Brahma Mutt
Sriperambudur	The Ubhayavedanta Sanskrit College

Srirangam	The Srirangam Devasthanam Library
Chennai	Fort St. George Museum
Chennai	International Institute of Tamil Studies
Madurai	School Historical Studies, Madurai Kamaraj University

Uttar Pradesh

Pithoragarh	Advaita Ashram, Mayavati
Rampur	Rampur Raza LIbrary
Varanasi	Banaras Hindu University, BKB
Vrindavan	Vrindavan Research Institute
Varanasi	Sarasvati Bhawan Library
Allahabad	Ganganath Jha Ken. Sanskrit Vidyapith
Leh(Laddak)	Central Institute of Buddhist Studies
Lucknow	Up State Archieves
Allahabad	Up State Regional Archieves
Allahabad	Govt. Manuscripts Library
Jhansi	Bundelkhand University Library
Haridwar	Gurukul Kanfri Viswavidyalaya Library
Khairangarh	Indira Kala Sangita Viswavidyalaya
Lucknow	Tagore Library Lucknow Univesity
Dehradun	Anthropological Survey of India Library (North-Western)
Varanasi	Nagari Pracharini Sabha
Lucknow	Akhil Bharatiya Sanskrit Parishad
Aligarh	Maulana Azad Library,, Aligarh Muslim University
Deoband	Darul Uloom (Deoband) Library
Lucknow	Kutub-Khana-E-Asiriya.
Lucknow	Nadwatul Ulma
Lucknow	Darul Uloom firangi Mahal

Lucknow	Madarsa-ul-Waizin
Lucknow	Jamiya Nazemiya
Meerut	Jamia Mansasiya
Lucknow	Sultan Ul-Madaris
Saharanpur	Mazhirul-Uloom
Rampur	Madarsa Aliya
Muradabad	Jamia Qazimiya Madarsa Mir
Amroha	Jamia-Islamia Arabia
Varanasi	Madaarsatul Islah Sarai Mir
Mubarakpur	Jamiya Arabiya Ihyaul Uloom
Maunathbanjan	Jamiya Mitlahul-Uloom
Maunathbanjan	Madarsa Islamiya Arabiya Darul Uloom
Barielly	Madarsa Manzarul Islam
Hatwai	Jamia Arabia
Dabhel	Jamia-Arabia Talimud-Din
Roude	Jamia Husainiya
Varanasi	Sri S R Gayakwad Library
Varanasi	Geonka Sanskrit Mahavidhyalaya Library
Lucknow	Amruddaul public Library
Banda	Chandan Das Sahitya Sodgsansthan
Bhadeni, banareș	Sri Syadvada Digambar Jain Mahavidhyalaya
Azamgarh	Darul Musannefin (Shibli Academy)
Dehradun	Dr. Balvir Singh Sahitya Kendra
Jhansi	Government Museum
Allahabad	Hindi Sahitya Sammelan (Hindu Sangrahalay)
Agra	Kanhaiyalal Maniklal Munshi Hindu & Atha Bharavijnanan Vidyapith
Gorakhpur	Nagarjun Buddhist Foundation

Aliganj, Etah	The Bhandara of Santinatha Jain Temple
Allahabad	Rajakiya Pandulipi Pustakalaya
Garhi, Aligarh	Syed Khairat Ali Library (I Dada-I-Hamadaniya)
Qamarabad	Darul Salam
Hapur	Sri Ambedkar Pustakalaya, Shahid Ramsaroop Jatav marg
Kashirampur (Kapli)	P K Lok Vikas Samsthan
Sikkim	
Gangtok	Sikkim Research Institute of Tibetology
West Begal	
Calcutta	Asiatic Society
Calcutta	National Library
Calcutta	Sri Chaitanya Research Institute
Calcutta	Vishwa Bharti Library
Calcutta	Ravindra Bharti Library
Calcutta	Calcutta Madras
Calcutta	Geothals Library
Darjeeling	Mss Section, Deptt. of Bengali, North Bengal University
Calcutta(Behala)	Indira Calcutta Organisation
Calcutta	Jain Bhawan, Kalakar Street
Culcutta	Jain Bhawan, Kalakar Street
Burdhman	University of Burdhman, Rajbati
Calcutta	Calcutta Sanskrit College
Calcutta	Bangiya Sahitya Parishad
Nadiad	The Dahilaksmi library
Rangpur	The Rangpur Sahitya Parishad
Calcutta	Mahabodhi Society of Indira, College

	Square
Navadwipa, Calcutta	Navedwip public Library
Nabadwip	Nabadwipa Sadharana Granthakara
Calcutta	Sanskrit Sahitya Parishat (Raja Dinendra Street)
Serampore	Serampore Colege
Calcutta	State Archives of West Bengal
Calcutta	University of Calcutta

Source: IGNCA© 1999

There may be many more institutions and individuals in the country possessing collections of Oriental books and manuscripts. It is hoped that they will also be known to the world if efforts in this direction are continued.

INDEX